HOW TO
ENJOY THE BIBLE

THE PEOPLE'S LIBRARY

HODDER AND STOUGHTON LIMITED
ST. PAUL'S HOUSE, LONDON, E.C.4

HOW TO
ENJOY THE BIBLE

BY

ANTHONY C. DEANE

CANON OF WINDSOR AND
CHAPLAIN TO H.M. THE KING

LONDON
HODDER & STOUGHTON LIMITED

First published	.	.	.	January	1925
Reprinted	.	.	.	March	1925
Reprinted	.	.	.	April	1925
Reprinted	.	.	.	June	1925
Reprinted	.	.	.	October	1925
Reprinted	.	.	.	March	1926
Reprinted	.	.	.	January	1927
Reprinted	.	.	.	February	1928
Reprinted	.	.	.	November	1929
Reprinted	.	.	.	February	1933
Reprinted	.	.	.	February	1935
Reprinted	.	.	.	October	1937

PRINTED AND BOUND IN GREAT BRITAIN FOR HODDER & STOUGHTON, LTD., BY RICHARD CLAY & SONS, LTD., BUNGAY, SUFFOLK.

CONTENTS

PART ONE
PRELIMINARY THOUGHTS

PART TWO
SUGGESTIONS FOR READING

v

CONTENTS

PART ONE
PRELIMINARY THOUGHTS

PART TWO
SUGGESTIONS FOR READING

PART ONE
PRELIMINARY THOUGHTS

I

I⊤ were needless to justify the title of this book but for the confused thought which counts joy the foe of reverence, opposes religion to pleasure, and identifies seriousness with gloom. Yet, this being an old and persisting error, which haunts most of us in some degree, let us face it squarely and master it at the outset. That must be done before we can go on our way through the Bible rejoicing, without a tremor lest our enjoyment dishonour its worth or lessen its spiritual potency.

Beyond question, the Bible has in it writings which every Christian holds, in a unique sense, sacred. I should stray beyond the scope of this volume if I attempted to discuss here the precise meaning, nature, and limits of " inspiration." That is a problem of theology, a theme of often beclouded dispute, with which, for our present purpose, we need not concern ourselves. Enough to agree—as all accepting the Christian religion in any form will do—that, in every sense, here are pages inspired beyond all other writings. They bestow our knowledge of God, our hope in man, our interpretation of life, our faith in triumph over death. We cannot read them without profound awe. But why must we suppose awe to exclude delight? After all, it has been those pure and devout souls of each age who held the Scriptures in deepest reverence that found also in them their most satisfying pleasure. And the reason is clear. They knew what we all profess to believe— that to every Christian the Bible message is good tidings of great joy. But how odd a custom, how strangely perverted a reverence, is the convention which bids us read tidings of great joy with looks of sombre dejection! In a place of worship a stranger might not readily suppose, either from the reader's voice or the listeners' faces, that a message of joy was being delivered. Even commerce seems to have been infected with the same idea. You enter a bookshop. Amidst its wealth of colour, you ask for a Bible. It will be strange indeed if the happiest book in the world is not offered you in a binding of funereal black.

We need, then, to get clear from all such false notions of reverence, which in fact dishonour what they are meant to extol. Believing that the Bible is, in a special sense, a divine gift to man, we must believe that it was given for man's happiness.

It was meant for enjoyment, and he who fails to enjoy it fails to use it rightly. We need not forget its solemnity of warning when we find it the most radiant of all books. It brightens what else were inexplicable darkness. It brings the noblest thought in noblest speech. It teaches, it inspires, it consoles, it heartens. Have we not here fit cause of enjoyment?

If this enjoyment be of many kinds, to that which is, in the narrower sense, spiritual, the others are not hostile but contributory. He who thinks these writings uniquely inspired does not find that their solace for his soul is lessened when he has studied their history, or allows himself to revel in their magnificence as poetry and prose. Most of us feel that our powers of prayer in some great cathedral are helped, not hindered, if we have trained ourselves to appreciate its beauty of architecture. We need not fear loss of spiritual profit from the Bible because we revere and enjoy it as superb literature. And, conversely, it has happened often that a reader drawn to the Bible at the first by its literary splendour alone has ended by finding in it something beyond all literature. The Bible itself convinces when " apologetics " about the Bible fail. The portrait merges in a Person : the Word (we may say in all reverence) becomes Flesh.

II

There can be no doubt, unhappily, that to-day the English are not a Bible-reading people, as were their ancestors. We may concede that in the past much of the reading was unintelligent or perfunctory, done as a prescribed act of virtue. Even so, it brought the readers certain gains, of which one was an acquaintance with the finest literature in their tongue. And a result of disuse becomes clear when we set together the fustian often written by " educated " people now and the prose of humble folk (let Bunyan serve as instance) whose memories were stored with the idiom of the Authorized Version. None the less, there are pleasant signs of a quickened taste for English literature. We may observe the bettered teaching of it at schools and universities, the popular lectures, the cheap editions of great books, the throngs using public libraries not merely for trivialities of the moment. So much the stranger, then, must seem this new habit of leaving the Bible unread, for with less loss the student of English letters might ignore Shakespeare.

This " decline of Bible-reading " has become a frequent theme at Church congresses and conferences. Some of its causes are obvious. There are others which had best be left undiscussed in this book, meant to bring its readers into the sunshine of the Bible, not into the acrid fog of ecclesiastical controversy. But there remain points of another kind which we ought to consider. And the first is a truth which sounds like a paradox : namely, that a large part of the blame for the neglect of the Bible must fall upon people who do not neglect it.

For, unconsciously enough, they encourage false ideas. They are apt to read furtively, as loth to parade an act of constrained virtue ; they read as a task enjoined rather than a delight enjoyed. Again, it is upon the " duty " of reading the Bible that preachers insist ; most frequently (and most mischievously) when they face young people. Accepting this view, presently some of their hearers will sit down to read, in the prospect of a drear ten minutes, to be endured for conscience' sake. Having been led to expect boredom, the chances are that they will find it. Why do not our preachers declare boldly that the Bible is the most enjoyable volume in the world ; that, if to read it is a duty, not to read it is to miss a thrilling pleasure ? Here, again, the most likely cause is a wrong theory of reverence, hindering these preachers from saying in public (possibly even from allowing themselves to think in private !) that the Bible is not only the most spiritually helpful, or the noblest, but also the most fascinating of books. After all, though, their laudable aim is to get the Bible read, and mere insistence upon the " duty " is unlikely to have a very large result. They may retort that, anyhow, people cannot enjoy the Bible unless they read it. This is rather obviously true. Yet it is equally true that the great mass of people to-day will not begin to read the Bible unless they expect to enjoy it.

And I am sure that we who do value it should be less shamefaced in using it. Of the many kinds of reading, some—the close technical study and the devout meditation—must be done in solitude. But there is no reason why enjoyment of great literature should be secret, or why we should blush, as if detected in some cloaked act of piety, to be found with an open Bible before us. In an hour of leisure we might take up this as un-affectedly as we turn for refreshment to any other great work. There are many right ways of reverencing the Bible, but to treat it strictly as an article of bedroom furniture is not one of them.

And this swifter, more general kind of reading— distinct both from devotional meditation and critical study—is really needed to supplement the others. We cannot value the Scriptures rightly without it. We may be interested in some textual question, or examine, with the help of comment-

aries, some abstruse passage in an effort to elucidate the meaning. Or we may ponder deeply
some words which seem to touch our inmost
lives, and shape the thoughts into prayer. Or,
following the excellent practice of our ancestors,
we may make a habit of " reading our chapter "
daily. Yet we shall never feel the true force of
(let us say) Job, or the Acts, or a Gospel or
Epistle, simply by studying it piecemeal, a few
verses or even a chapter at a time. We must read
through the whole book at a sitting. Its cumula-
tive effect, experienced by this means, is something
apart from, and transcending, the series of
impressions derived from the chapters taken
separately. Not only then is the literary splendour
of the book made clear, so that we gain a new
delight from the reading, but also we realize for
the first time the book's soul, its inmost character.
If hitherto we have limited ourselves to small
portions, an hour of this swifter yet unhurried
reading, as we sit at leisure by the fireside, may
mark the beginning of that rich enjoyment which
the Bible is meant to give.

III

I pass to another reason often alleged for the
" decline in Bible-reading."

We are told that it is less read to-day because the Higher Criticism has weakened its historical trustworthiness and, consequently, its spiritual authority. Writers in the popular Press, where these statements are rather frequent, seem seldom to know what " Higher Criticism " really means. It is perhaps an ill-chosen, but merely technical term. " Lower Criticism " concerns itself with textual study, striving to restore the documents to their original wording; " higher criticism " examines the history of the documents and of their writers. Its name is intended to distinguish it from, but not to claim any superiority over, textual criticism. Moreover, " higher criticism " should not be confused with " modernism," which again is distinct from " rationalism."

But I need not waste time upon these arid abstract terms, the most of which are blots upon our language and lead, as the name " higher criticism " has led, to confusion of thought. What seems incontestably true is that some folk to-day are disquieted by the supposed results of biblical criticism. They profess no close acquaintance with it, but believe vaguely that it has shaken the credit of the Scriptures. Because such misgivings mar the enjoyment of Bible-reading, let it be said plainly here that they are baseless. If modern expert study has changed beliefs about the Bible, it has also deepened faith in the Bible. It has taken away difficulties which long had perplexed every thoughtful reader. It has given new perspective, new interest, new intelligibility, new richness. To-day the Bible is not less divine because it seems also more human. Its claim to be the witness of eternal truth has been strengthened. Its foundations have been tested as have been those of no other work, and they endure. Our knowledge of the New Testament, in particular, has been increased vastly by the work of scholars within the last thirty years. To their toil is due the fact that to-day it can be read by us with more spiritual profit, more understanding, and more enjoyment than were possible for our predecessors.

To say this is to have in mind points upon which virtually all scholars have reached agreement, conclusions which seem now to be established beyond serious cavil. Other points are in dispute still; some, perhaps, always to remain dubitable. Indeed, critics are not exempt from the foible of setting forth as accepted and incontrovertible facts what are, at best, but plausible surmises. There are rash theories; there are views which after a seeming triumph have to be replaced again by others too quickly judged obsolete; there are speculations which rest upon personal prejudgment rather than upon evidence. Many critics, for example, have thought to simplify belief by expunging the supernatural from Scripture records, only to find that this process creates difficulties more formidable than any it was designed to relieve. Yet, when all such cautions have been uttered and deductions made, there does remain a store of enduring value which has been won by modern research for modern readers.

For instance, perplexity might well destroy our chances of enjoyment were we still asked to believe every sentence in the Bible to be " the word of God," and therefore of equal value, authority, and interest. By that reckoning, a page of Leviticus would have the same importance as a page of Luke.[1] Of course the doctrine of " verbal inspiration," in its extreme form, has been discarded long since, yet the relics of its influence still deter many people from recognizing frankly the immense inequalities of the Bible. We are apt even now to extol it as though it were a single book, and to speak of its " characteristics." But it is a book only in the material sense that it brings some eighty documents within one binding.

[1] For the sake of clearness, in this volume " St." will be prefixed to the name of an Evangelist when the reference is to the man, but omitted when the reference is to the book. Thus, " St. Luke " will signify the Physician and Evangelist; " Luke," the Third Gospel.

It is difficult to find a single characteristic common to all these documents, unless it be a consciousness of God—and even that is not explicit in quite all. In every other way they are amazingly varied. It is not merely that some are separated from others by vast intervals of date. They differ in subject, treatment, point-of-view, character, and value. The gulf is as wide at times as that dividing (let us say) a poem by Keats from a set of public health regulations issued by the Ministry of Health.

This being so, what were more foolish than a pretence that we ought to derive equal pleasure from every part of the Bible, or to maintain of some parts that, for the general reader, they have any interest at all? We are not (let us say it frankly) bound in conscience to struggle with mere lists of names, or genealogies, or detailed sanitary enactments, merely because they happen to lie between the same covers as things so magnificent as the Book of Job and the Gospel of John. But in the Bible are history, drama, folklore, lyrical poetry, idyll, philosophy, meditation, personal narrative, letters, tracts for the times— literature of almost every kind, so that at any moment we can turn to something which chimes with our mood. In reading for enjoyment we shall not open the pages at random, or follow the example of our forefathers, who plodded their difficult way, missing no word, from the first page of Genesis to the last of Revelation. From time to time we shall choose one book for our delight, knowing that one book differeth from another book in glory. At every turn we shall be helped by the fuller knowledge which modern study of the Bible has put at our service. We shall be free from theories of mechanical inspiration and from moral perplexities which, probably enough, hindered our Bible-reading in our youth. As we understand better both the books themselves and the circumstances in which they were written, our right of enjoyment will grow more clear.

And, so far as we can read with an alert mind and a quickened literary sense, we may ourselves contribute to this task of right interpretation. Critical problems, even when they are concerned with questions of date, authorship, and genuineness, are not to be solved by technical scholarship alone. The judgment of academic scholars, despite their equipment of learning, often goes astray because they lack that which many a general reader can supply. For example, the point in question may be whether some record is the testimony of an eye-witness, or was put together at a later time, partly from earlier accounts, and partly from pious imaginings of the writer. Details of grammar, idiom, and vocabulary, signs of divergence from, or resemblance to, other records will be noted by scholars, and discussed by them eagerly. When (which happens less often than one could wish) they agree in the conclusions they draw, these become of great importance. Yet, while he will not be so foolish as to disregard them, the reader with a trained literary sense—especially if he has himself attempted creative work in literature—will prefer to base his judgment on evidence of another kind. He may lack knowledge of Greek particles, but he is keenly sensitive to nuances of style. And his instinct will make him feel—indefinably but convincingly—whether or no the record rings true, whether it be the fruit of reflective imaginings or is a compilation from other documents, or an observed transcript from life. Without undervaluing the work of scholars, it may be said that many a question of biblical criticism has been decided by them with insufficient regard to evidence of the kind which men of letters (in the wider meaning) can discern. Our Revised Version of the New Testament showed how separate great biblical erudition may be from the literary sense! Possibly enough, then, the general reader's enjoyment of the Bible, limited as his technical scholarship seems, may reach far. To use an imperfect analogy, some of the most enlightening books on Shakespeare have come from writers who certainly were Shakespeare-lovers but not at all technical Shakespearean experts. Somewhat in the same way, if men and women of culture would spend more time and thought upon their Bibles, the results, I believe, often would benefit not themselves alone. Supplementing, from a different angle, the work of the specialists, studies written by such Bible-readers might reach a wide public and have a distinctive value.

IV

But this is a hope for the future. At present most English people need still to be shown their right to enjoy and the right enjoyment. Of the former point something has been said in this chapter, and I do not think this right to enjoy need be vindicated at greater length. What deters those who hesitate over it is not a reasoned misgiving but a vague sentiment. In truth, this fear that we may dishonour or " secularize " the Bible by looking for frank and human delight when we read it is simply an unhappy inheritance from an unhappy perversion of Christianity. Let us shake ourselves free from it once for all. The right to enjoy is clear.

What may be less clear are the means of gaining this enjoyment; and to make suggestions about them, showing how they may be applied to the various parts of the Bible, is the chief purpose of this book. For the most part it will try to make vivid that special joy to be won by reading the Bible comprehensively, as great literature. But I must not therefore be supposed to undervalue those kindred yet different joys which come from devotional reading and from precise study. The joy of devotional reading, at our best moments, when a divine message stirs our whole being and fills us with the overmastering sense of God's nearness and love—this is a joy so intimate and sacred that it may not be set down in words. Very real, too, is the deep satisfaction of the student as, strengthening his own knowledge with stores of learning others have put at his service, he pores over some abstruse passage until he feels that, for the first time, its precise meaning has become clear to him. That, indeed, is a pleasure which, in some degree, we all should know. There are writings in the Bible (the Galatian letter and some prophetical books may stand as examples) a general reading of which can hardly give enjoyment, unless we have studied beforehand those circumstances which caused them to be written and coloured their every sentence.

But it is of general reading that, in the main, I must be content to speak; almost it might be termed " casual," did not that epithet admit of a wrong interpretation. Yet casual reading need not be careless. Let us suppose that the day's work is done. We settle down to read. We are out of tune, it may be, for laborious study, yet would not spend all our leisure over the newspaper or books of the moment. It is in this mood that we turn most readily to some great work of the past. And it is then that, quite naturally, in place of some other classic, we might take up our Bible. At the start that may need some little effort of the will. Soon the enjoyment will prove so keen that to read will be less difficult than to make an end of reading. We shall have learned by practical experience how to enjoy the Bible.

Let me add one immediate word of prosaic yet necessary counsel. We cannot expect much pleasure from pages the reading of which is a physical strain. In other words, we must obtain, if we have it not, a Bible well printed on good paper. For choice, let it be without the distracting margin of references. At least it must not be one of those which seem to have been fashioned in the interests of oculists and opticians. Many people, not impoverished, are strangely content with Bibles in a type they would not tolerate for any other book they loved. Yet this of all books is the most companionable, and this, beyond any other, should come to us in noble form.

CHAPTER II

THE CHARM OF THE
ENGLISH BIBLE

I

THE English Bible is the chief glory of English prose. Through three centuries no other work has had a comparable influence on our creed and thought, on our speech and literature. We are accustomed to think this pre-eminence due to the intrinsic and sacred character of its contents, to the fact that it brings man his knowledge of God. This is obviously true. Also it is true, and perhaps less obvious, that our Bible might have held the same message, have translated the originals with equal faithfulness, yet never have gained a like place in people's hearts. For it might have been done with ample care and learning, yet in such a way as to lack charm. How possible this is grows clear when we pass to other renderings. We can admire the sonorous monotony of the Vulgate. We cannot love it. We can applaud the exact precision of some modern English versions. But they leave us cold. It is the charm of the English Bible that has endeared it through centuries to all sorts and conditions of men. And if charm be a quality eluding final analysis, we may be sure that here, among its contributing parts, are simplicity, an unmatched happiness of diction, rhythms changing in exquisite accord with the sense, lucid reverence, and tender gentleness.

To praise the English Bible is, for most of us, to have in mind the Authorized Version. Though no praise of it could be too high, some bestowed by modern critics has been misdirected. They speak as though the English Bible had been created, as it were, by those forty-seven divines who, at James the First's bidding, toiled at it between 1604 and 1611. What they did make, to their undying credit, was the Authorized Version—a version, by the way, which, despite its title-page, seems never to have been authorized by king, parliament, or convocation. Its own merit gained it authority, and soon it had dispossessed all rivals. Yet the English Bible was not the product of these few years, but the growth of (to be precise) eighty-six. It began, that is to say, with the New Testament of William Tyndale in 1525; it culminated in the Authorized Version of 1611. And if the chief share in it must be ascribed to any one worker, Tyndale is the man.

27

Parts of Scripture had been set forth in the vernacular from Saxon days onwards. The first complete Bible in English was made soon after 1380 by followers of Wyclif—it seems proven that he himself had no share in it. This was a translation of a translation; a rendering made not from the original Hebrew and Greek, but from the Latin Vulgate. Tyndale was the first to work directly from the originals. His own explicit statement shows that he did not consult any Wyclifite version; in fact, he possessed none. His English was his own, an immediate rendering from the Greek manuscripts. The life of Tyndale belongs to English history, and need not be retold in detail here—how, forbidden licence to do his work in England, he began its accomplishment abroad; how, like other early translators, he jeopardized both himself and his book by marginal notes aggressive with the ecclesiastical and civil polemic of his own day; how copies of his New Testament, smuggled into England, were bought with an equal eagerness by those anxious to read and those anxious to suppress; how he had but lately begun upon the Old Testament when he was put to death. By that time (1536) no fewer than seven different issues of his complete New Testament had been printed, as well as a translation of the Pentateuch.

Though Tyndale died with his own version unfinished, he had wrought enduring service to all others. He had used a style and idiom exactly suited to the English Bible. He had set a pattern of flexible and lucid prose, of wonderful rhythm, of cadence and euphony, which all subsequent translators had the wisdom to follow. When they were at work upon the New Testament, they reproduced Tyndale's version with the least change that seemed necessary. When they translated Old Testament books which he had left undone, they strove to write as nearly as possible in his fashion. In the year of his death came Coverdale's Bible; in 1537 that bearing the fictitious name of "Matthew." "The Great Bible" (from which comes the Prayer-book version of the Psalms) appeared in 1539, the "Genevan" in 1560, the "Bishops' Bible" in 1568. And the first rule adopted by those summoned to prepare the Bible of 1611 was "the Bishops' Bible to be followed, and as little altered as the truth of the original will permit." Thus through these eighty-six years the Tyndale tradition persisted, being handed on from one translation to the next. Often, too, the makers of the Authorized Version modified the Bishops' Bible by a direct return to the wording of Tyndale himself. When sentences had wholly to be recast,

29

in almost every instance the new translation bettered the old, but never did it depart from the standard of rhythm and euphony which Tyndale had set up.

Profoundly grateful, then, as we are to that company of divines, we should be yet more grateful for what they did not do and so easily might have done. They might have set aside the Tyndale tradition as archaic, and replaced its exquisite simplicity of phrasing by that tumid prose in which they themselves excelled. The extremely diffuse " Preface " to the Authorized Version, written by one of them (Miles Smith, afterwards Bishop of Gloucester), is omitted— doubtless by reason of its length—from modern reprints of the Bible. But the translators' dedication [1] of their work to King James can be found still in every copy. Let us recall its opening sentences :—

Great and manifold were the blessings, most dread Sovereign, which Almighty God, the Father of all mercies, bestowed upon us the people of England, when first He

[1] There is no contemporary record, I believe, about the authorship of the Dedication. But I incline to suspect that it came from the same hand as the Preface. In the Preface, Mr. Smith (rather appropriately) observes that the translators " did not disdain to bring back to the anvil that which we had hammered." The Dedication derides " selfconceited brethren liking nothing but what is hammered on their anvil."

sent Your Majesty's Royal Person to rule and reign over us. For whereas it was the expectation of many, who wished not well unto our Sion, that upon the setting of that bright Occidental Star, Queen Elizabeth of most happy memory, some thick and palpable clouds of darkness would so have overshadowed this Land, that men should have been in doubt which way they were to walk ; and that it should hardly be known, who was to direct the unsettled State ; the appearance of Your Majesty, as of the Sun in his strength, instantly dispelled those supposed and surmised mists. . . .

We are yet some way from the end of the sentence. It contains 131 words. But there is no need to quote further. " Supposed and surmised mists " indeed ! Suppose (and surmise) that the makers of the Authorized Version, in place of conserving loyally the Tyndale tradition, had rendered the Bible in the English of their own choice—the English in which they cast their Dedication ! We may be glad that they had the good sense to keep their work in line with what had been done before. They knew that the English folk would resent a violent change of idiom. They knew that many a pellucid phrase, handed down from Tyndale through his successors, was already firm in the hearts of their countrymen. And they knew (to do them justice) that the sonorous and grandiloquent style they themselves admired, though it might adorn a Dedication, would not serve well to translate the Bible. They were

31

faithful to the old style. They brought in no word foreign to it. They used it so well that actually they increased its beauty. Thus the Authorized Version brought to a supreme height the charm of the English Bible.

II

Before we pass to a closer scrutiny of that charm, let us examine briefly some later translations. The Revised Version of the New Testament was published in 1881. The reasons for making it were ample. Scholarship had advanced notably since King James's days. Not only was the idiom of the Greek Testament understood better, but very early and important manuscripts had been discovered since 1611. Immense pains were spent upon the new work. As the seventeenth-century divines had resolved to change as little as they might the wording of the sixteenth-century " Bishops' Bible," so again the nineteenth-century revisers promised " to introduce as few changes as possible, consistently with faithfulness." But the average reader, having found this excellent principle affirmed in the preface, was the more dismayed when he turned to the body of the work. He was puzzled to reconcile the promise with the performance. He found changes on every page; almost in every sentence. Some, doubtless, had been compelled by the weight of new evidence from early manuscripts. Some were clear gain, making lucid sense of what hitherto had been obscure. Yet a large proportion seemed almost inconceivably needless and futile. Let us consider one or two instances from hundreds. The Authorized Version, in translating the account of Stephen's trial, had the phrase " all that sat in the council looking stedfastly on him." The Revisers altered *" looking stedfastly on him "* to *" fastening their eyes on him."* True, the change was harmless, but what imaginable gain could it bring?

Apart from very numerous alterations of this sort, the merely inept, were others worse by far. *" If thy hand offend thee,"* the Authorized Version ran; *" if thy hand cause thee to stumble,"* said the Revised—and pedantry bordered on absurdity. Most calamitous of all was the fact that the Revisers, skilled in Greek, had little ear for English. They showed themselves insensible of the verbal felicities, the rhythm, cadence, and euphony which were the chief glories of King James's Bible; which, indeed, had set it before any other work in English prose. At this time of day we need not enlarge upon this melancholy failure;

one specimen of its results will suffice. How exquisitely in tune with the meaning is the English of the fourteenth and three succeeding chapters of the Fourth Gospel! *"Let not your heart be troubled, neither let it be afraid."* If that most comfortable word be read slowly, we shall feel how its music enhances the effect. After the sudden movement of " troubled " there comes a pause, and then, at the close, the expectant ear finds rest in the second syllable of " afraid." Its stressed, open vowels, rounded off by the final consonant, seem to end the sentence on a note of tranquil strength. Let us read it once more, with a just emphasis upon that closing syllable: *" Let not your heart be troubled, neither let it be afraid."* Now contrast the Revised Version: *" Let not your heart be troubled, neither let it be fearful."* The whole effect is ruined! Under what pretext was it sacrificed? " Afraid " is a good enough word, of one meaning. " Fearful " has two, and in this place must be given the rarer sense, a sense in which the great majority of Bible-readers never use it.

Small wonder, then, that hard things were said of the Revised Version of the New Testament, or that the most of them were deserved. Yet, grave as these faults are, they should not lead us to consider the Version worthless. It does correct many mistranslations; it does elucidate many passages—especially in the Pauline Epistles—which the older translations had left dark. Therefore, though it cannot replace the Authorized Version, it supplements it. Often the general reader will profit by consulting it, using it, in fact, as a simple form of commentary.

We need to remember that much of the common censure applied to the Revised Version of the Bible goes wide of the mark because it does not discriminate. The faults of the Revised New Testament are indeed as evident as they are lamentable. But we should not fall into the error of supposing the Revised Old Testament to be a part of the same work, and therefore of the same poor quality. It was done by other hands, published three years later, and is vastly better. Here, for the first time, the poetical books in the Old Testament were printed as poems, and distinguished from the prose. And its makers took pains, as the New Testament Revisers had not, to maintain the level of style and idiom reached by their predecessors. While they did this with great success, they also brought meaning into many passages which had been quite unintelligible. Both points can be illustrated from the 28th chapter of Job. The later part—that beginning with verse 12: "*But where shall wisdom be*

found ? And where is the place of understanding ? "
is, by common consent, to be reckoned among the
most magnificent things in the Bible. It is glorious
in the Authorized Version; it is no less glorious
in the Revised. The verbal changes are few, and
not one of them brings in a discordant word or
mars the superb rhythm. The first eleven verses
of the chapter give a contrasting picture. We
know (such is their thought) where man's material
treasures are to be found. It is from the depths
of the earth that he digs his silver, and gold, and
iron.

> *Surely there is a mine for silver,*
> *And a place for gold which they refine,*
> *Iron is taken out of the earth . . .*

and in the next two verses is a vivid description
of the miner at work. But it is blurred hopelessly
by the Authorized translation :

> *He setteth an end to darkness, and searcheth out all*
> *perfection : the stones of darkness, and the shadow of*
> *death.*
> *The flood breaketh out from the inhabitant ; even the*
> *waters forgotten of the foot : they are dried up, they are*
> *gone away from men.*

We may wonder what sense this tangle of words
had for the translators who wrote it. But here

is the real meaning, given us by the Revised
Version :

Man setteth an end to darkness,
And searcheth out to the furthest bound
The stones of thick darkness and of the shadow of death.
He breaketh open a shaft away from where men sojourn ;
They are forgotten of the foot that passeth by ;
They hang afar from men, they swing to and fro.

So, in place of words without meaning, we have
this unforgettable picture of the mines. It is
continued in the verses that follow. Those
underground paths are unseen by birds, however
keen their vision, are untrodden by beast. But
man in his quest of the earth's treasures attacks
the flinty walls, overturns mountains, cuts passages through the rock, dams the subterranean
streams, brings the hidden things to light. By
such toil he wins his riches; in the depths of the
earth he finds them. But where shall wisdom be
found? And where is the place of understanding?
So we are led up intelligibly to the splendid and
familiar passage that begins with those words,
culminating gloriously :

When He made a decree for the rain,
And a way for the lightning of the thunder :
Then did He see it, and declare it ;
He established it, yea, and searched it out.
And unto man He said,
Behold, the fear of the Lord, that is wisdom ;
And to depart from evil is understanding.

37

It would be easy to give a score of like examples, to each of which the Revised Old Testament brought point and meaning without any loss of euphony. We must not class it, then, with the Revised New Testament. For the reading of the Old Testament—and of the Apocrypha also—we should use, beyond doubt, the Revised Version.

III

Since the Revised Version was published, a number of independent translations of the New Testament have been made by scholars who frankly abandoned the diction inherited from Tyndale, replacing it by "modern English." [1] When we examine any of these works our first (and rather laudable) instinct may be to dismiss it as an outrage. Its pedestrian language seems ruthlessly to have destroyed the Bible's charm; this, we feel, is many degrees worse than the Revised Version. Yet the writers can urge points in defence which we should not ignore: (i) that the abundant new light thrown on New Testament

---

[1] Some of the best known are: *The New Testament in Modern Speech*, by Dr. Weymouth, *The Twentieth Century New Testament*, *The New Testament: A new translation*, by Dr. James Moffatt, and *The New Testament: an American translation*, by Dr. Goodspeed.

Greek since the Revised Version was made justifies a new translation; (ii) that the rhythm and dignity of the traditional rendering, attractive though they are, have no equivalent in the originals which they translate; the Greek of the New Testament, as modern discoveries have proved, was the colloquial form of the age in which it was written, and therefore is translated best by colloquial English; (iii) that such a rendering, done in the spoken English of everyday life, reproduces for us as nearly as possible the kind of impression which the New Testament books must have made upon their first readers.

Undoubtedly these pleas have weight. Yet the reader may retort that, while he would not demur to the use of modern English, the idiom actually employed by these books is too often not English at all, either ancient or modern, but an intolerable jargon. And he will resent wanton changes, changes where there is neither archaic word to be modernized nor obscurity of meaning to be cleared. It must seem an odd taste, for instance, which finds a need of altering "*Jesus wept*" into "*Jesus shed tears*" (Dr. Goodspeed) or "*Jesus burst into tears*" (Dr. Moffatt). Exasperating, however, as are such futilities, they need not blind us to the real value of these modernized translations for many people. Dr. Moffatt's, despite its flaws, is the most scholarly of them. When used rightly, not to replace but to supplement the Authorized Version, I have found often that it gives the general reader precisely the help he needs. He is not expert in Hellenistic Greek, we may suppose, and lacks time for the study of elaborate commentaries. By consulting Dr. Moffatt's translation when he reads, for instance, a Pauline Epistle, he will have the results of modern scholarship to aid him. He will be able far better than before to follow the steps of St. Paul's argument, and to understand the meaning of passages which are quite cryptic in the Authorized Version and by no means pellucid in the Revised. The "parallel edition" is specially convenient, which prints side by side the Authorized Version and Dr. Moffatt's. The best method, I believe, is to read through several chapters in the Authorized Version; then to read through Dr. Moffatt's rendering of them, and finally to read them once more in the older form. The first reading will remind us of their spiritual fire and literary charm. The second, though in language needlessly debased, will make clear the sequence of thought. And in the third reading both pleasures will commingle, giving keen enjoyment. If indeed the reader have literary sense, this direct contrast with "modern English" will make him revere more than ever the beauty of the Authorized Version. And that, too, will be gain.

Of the Old Testament, it is the poetical books which translators have sought most commonly to reproduce in modern idiom.[1] Many have tried their hands at the Psalms; no other has come near Dr. Cheyne's success. His small edition of *The Book of Psalms*, in Kegan Paul's "Parchment Library," was most valuable. I fear that it passed out of print long since, and that the second-hand shops must be searched for it. Professor McFadyen's *Isaiah in Modern Speech* and *Jeremiah in Modern Speech*[2] are skilful attempts to give not only a clear rendering, but something of the Hebrew rhythm. Mr. Mumford's *Job: a Metrical Version*,[3] is unexpectedly effective. Here, for example, are the opening verses of chapter xix in the Revised Version :

How long will ye vex my soul,
And break me in pieces with words ?
These ten times have ye reproached me :
Ye are not ashamed that ye deal hardly with me.
And be it indeed that I have erred,
Mine error remaineth with myself. . . .

[1] Since this chapter was written, Dr. Moffatt has produced a modernized translation of the complete Old Testament, in two volumes. (Hodder & Stoughton.)

[2] James Clarke, each 6s.

[3] Hodder & Stoughton, 6s.

Know now that God hath subverted me in my cause,
And hath compassed me with his net. . . .
He hath also kindled his wrath against me,
And he counteth me unto him as one of his adversaries.
His troops come on together and cast up their way against
*   me,*
And encamp round about my tent.
He hath put my brethren far from me,
And mine acquaintance are wholly estranged from me.

and here is Mr. Mumford's rendering :

How long will ye vex and afflict me ?   How long will ye
*   smite me with swords ?*
These ten times have ye reproached me, unashamed have
*   ye broke me with words ;*
And be it indeed I have erred, my blame is mine own,
*   nor forget*
It is God that subverteth his servant, and compassed me
*   round in his net. . . .*
He counteth me one of his foemen and kindleth his wrath
*   against me ;*
His troops like an army encircle, they encompass,
*   entrench as in war ;*
He parteth my brethren from me, mine acquaintance
*   he setteth afar.*

We may doubt if the Book of Job, as it stands in the Bible, needs the supplement of any " metrical version "; but we shall agree, I think, that, granted a need of it, Mr. Mumford has contrived it admirably, and with a faithfulness to the original text which is remarkable.

IV

Yet no new versions, however skilful and accurate, can have for us a charm like that of our historic English Bible. To that, with some sense of relief, we may return. We need not think the search irreverent which tries to find the secret of this charm. Apart from its sacred character, the Bible is dear to many of us because it is linked closely with memories of childhood. Its stories were among the first we heard. And this Book had entered deeply into the lives of our fathers before us, so that we, who may owe more of our mental habits than we guess to the past, have inherited not only the Bible itself but an aptitude for prizing it. We need not hesitate to admit also the charm of the English Bible as great literature, and to use this for heightening our enjoyment of it. I have protested already against the falsity of supposing that in this way we shall " secularize " our view of the Scriptures. After all, the power of transmuting the Bible from tongues so unlike our own into the noblest English was of the spirit— was, in the strictest sense, spiritual. To treat the Bible simply as a manual of English prose would be as shortsighted as to treat old churches simply as architectural museums. But to say

43

that we should not examine and revel in the splendour of the Bible as fine literature is as foolish as to deny ourselves the right of examining and enjoying fine architecture because it is within a church. To-day we need, by common consent, everything that will encourage people to read their Bibles, and to read them with eager enjoyment. Well, here is a most practical help for any who have found the reading irksome. Train yourself not merely to feel in a general way the Bible's literary charm, but to notice in detail how that charm is gained. What has made the wording of this sentence so extraordinarily effective? What gives that paragraph its perfection of rhythm? What were the methods of those who made this wonderful English? When we pass, in short, from saying " How fine this is ! " to asking " Why is this so fine ? " we put ourselves in the way of acquiring a new interest, of finding a new and inexhaustible pleasure in our reading. It will not lessen other and deeper pleasures. But it will help us to enjoy the Bible, and to feel more grateful to those whose careful art clothed its message in so magnificent a form.

Perhaps the simplest beginning is to notice how skilfully the translators chose their words from our rich twofold vocabulary. They prefer, for the most part, short words. They know the tranquil effect given by a flow of monosyllables :

Blessed are the pure in heart, for they shall see God—

and in Ruth, that idyll of the harvest field, how exactly the wording of this sentence matches the setting, enhances its simple grace :

The Lord do so to me, and more also, if ought but death part thee and me—

seventeen words, and only eighteen syllables. Try the result of recasting that in longer words, and observe how its tender charm is marred ! But no less well did these translators know how to employ sonorous Latinisms when a loftier diction was in better accord with the sense :

Now unto the King eternal, immortal, invisible . . .
This corruption shall put on incorruption, and this mortal shall put on immortality. . . .
Whiles by the experiment of this ministration they glorify God. . . .

Further, they knew, as did Shakespeare, the value for a special purpose of conjoining the two kinds of words, the Saxon and the Latin, or of dropping one Latin sonority into the midst of a Saxon sentence. Everyone knows the most striking example in Shakespeare :

> *the multitudinous seas incarnadine,*
> *Making the green one red.*

Not less fine, and not less deliberate, is the art which fashioned :

In the world ye shall have tribulation ; but be of good cheer ; I have overcome the world.

Now we shall find that modernized versions, with their too usual infelicity, have replaced " tribulation " in this sentence by " trouble." Doubtless " trouble " is a perfectly good word; a word often employed by the ancient translators. Why did they reject it here ? Why did they drop this sudden Latinism, this four-syllabled word, into the middle of their Saxon sentence ? Well, partly because its place *was* the middle; because, to make the sense vivid, to bring out the contrast between the world's portion and the victory of Christ, the reader should delay for an instant between the two contrasting clauses. ". . . . ye shall have trouble, but "—the sound does not compel a pause after " trouble." " Ye shall have tribulation, but "—that longer, more resonant word compels the pause after it which the sense demands. Again, that sudden Latinism grasps our attention. " In the world ye shall have tribulation " :—the word is ominous of coming ill, it rolls like far thunder. Then this dies into silence, and, in wonderful contrast, comes the serene calm of the Master's promise :

In the world ye shall have tribulation ;
But be of good cheer ; I have overcome the world.

Some readers may fear that all this is to
" reason too curiously," that our Bible translators
could not consciously have set themselves to
achieve these niceties of art. It is true enough
that they had no need to work out afresh the
principles of English prose when they met to
translate the Bible. Yet that was because they
were steeped in those principles already. A long
training of taste and ear enabled them by this
time almost instinctively to shape their sentences
well, to achieve their effects of rhythm and cadence,
to choose the one right word. But the art was
no less a real art because they had acquired it
long before, or had derived much of it from
predecessors. And such art is not to be mastered
without pains. Certainly none who themselves
have laboured to write English prose will believe
that the innumerable felicities of the English
Bible are so many happy accidents. Such handling
of consonants and vowels as we find in the
sentence :

The quiver rattleth against him, the glittering spear
and the shield,

is not due to chance.

What reader has not been thrilled by that

magnificent chapter describing how the Lord passed by before Elijah? A great and strong wind rent the mountains and brake in pieces the rocks; but the Lord was not in the wind: and after the wind an earthquake; but the Lord was not in the earthquake: and after the earthquake a fire; but the Lord was not in the fire: and after the fire " *a still small voice.*" Have we noticed how those two adjectives help the sense of contrast between hush and awe? Each has four consonants and but one pinched vowel-sound, and the " thick " double consonants at the beginning of each (*st, sm*) make them fall like separate drops of water. They compel you to speak them slowly, with a break between. Exchange them for: " *After the fire a quiet and gentle voice* "—and feel the difference !

Or let us recall a passage in a quite different key:

How often would I have gathered thy children together, even as a hen gathereth her chickens under her wings—

(a flow of nimble, lightly-stressed words, so fitting the picture that we seem to watch the chickens scurrying to their shelter. And then a check, an instantaneous change; slow, reluctant monosyllables, brimming with vain regret :)

and . . . ye . . . would . . . not !

48

Or listen to the prayer which Samson gasps as he lays his arms round the great pillars he is to shake into overthrow—and you can hear the labouring of his breath :

O Lord God, remember me, I pray thee, and strengthen me, I pray thee, only this once, O God, that I may be at once avenged of the Philistines. . . .

Is not that a triumph of art ?

But one might write chapters to praise these translators' astounding skill, alike in their choice of words and their control of rhythm. That rhythm you hear sometimes in a monotonous pulsing throb of lamentation :

Ye daughters of Israel, weep over Saul, who clothed you in scarlet, with other delights,—

and sometimes in a glorious ascent to a climax of triumphant faith :

Neither death, nor life, nor angels, nor principalities, nor powers, nor things present, nor things to come, nor height, nor depth, nor any other creature, shall be able to separate us from the love of God, which is in Christ Jesus our Lord.

The reader will find examples in plenty for himself. Merely I have tried to convince him, should he need conviction, that here is a means to aid us in enjoying the Bible. As we read, let us keep an open ear, alert to notice its verbal charm, its

D

unmatched felicity of style. And let us study these effects, noting the means, often so simple yet so astoundingly sure, by which they are achieved. When we have accustomed ourselves to do that, Bible-reading cannot seem an irksome task—and, as Dr. Johnson said, "what a man reads as a task will do him little good." Instead, we shall turn to the great literature of the Bible with inexhaustible delight. Yet this delight will be more than a merely æsthetic pleasure. Even apart from the profound sacredness of the Bible, its pages, like all great literature, are not only noble but ennobling. As we hear them, they charm and move us like great music. And, at the end, it is with a purged heart and a stouter resolve that we go forth again into the intricate bewilderment of the world.

PART TWO
SUGGESTIONS FOR READING

CHAPTER III   THE SYNOPTIC GOSPELS

I

HE is an unwise reader of the Bible who begins
it at the beginning. If we imagine one coming
to it for the first time, anxious to learn its message and to test its claims, we may feel that for
him the right point of departure would be the
Book of the Acts. Here he will find an historical
record of a new power at work in the world. It
not only revolutionized religion but transformed
man. Though Jewish in its origin, this was no
development of Judaism. On the contrary, it
declared war on the theory of racial exclusiveness
which lay at the heart of the Jewish creed. It
set the straitest Pharisee slaving for the Gentiles.
It propounded entirely new moral values. For its
sake frail men and women faced loss, persecution
and death with serene and happy courage.
Finally, it did more than change the whole
outlook upon life in this world: it brought a
triumphant certitude of what waits beyond.

Such are the facts of history which our reader

will learn from this book. The things happened. How did they happen? What had made them possible? These results, astounding but indubitable, must have had some proportionate cause. The Gospels were written to demonstrate what that cause was. From the Acts, then, our reader will pass in logical sequence to the Gospels. In their pages he finds a story which accounts adequately for the facts he has studied. Were this an imagined record, another satisfying explanation must be found. But there is no other, and this stands every test; this, for all its marvel, rings true. Having pondered with a wonder that deepens into awe, and rises into love, the words and works, the death and resurrection of Christ, our reader will feel that the story of the Gospels has answered the questions which the story of the Acts provoked. Then, his main quest achieved, he will learn from letters of early Christian days how the new belief was applied to problems of thought and conduct. After that it will be time enough for him to turn to the Old Testament. To read it before the New Testament would be to read it without the clue which changes it from a chance assemblage of ancient documents to a library selected with coherent purpose and meaning.

Such seems to be the course which a critical

student should follow who came newly to the Bible. First of all he should read the Acts of the Apostles, and then the Gospels. That sequence may be varied for the accustomed reader turning to his Bible for enjoyment. Yet he too should not read at random. He will have freed himself, let us hope, from the old illusion that everything in the Bible is (just because it is in the Bible) of the same quality and of a like importance. The New Testament has a value inexpressibly higher than the Old. And different parts of the New Testament are on different levels. There are books which were given place in it only after long hesitation and debate. Even if the ultimate decision were right, more than once it was based on theories of authorship, which now we know to be mistaken. It would be idle, for instance, to pretend that the second Epistle attributed to St. Peter has the same interest, spiritual authority, or literary worth as the first Epistle to the Corinthians. Far wider, of course, is the gulf between any Epistle and the Gospels. Few things would have dismayed St. Paul more than a knowledge that in times to come his words would be cited as infallible, and even be ranged, as of an equal authority, against the words of Christ himself. It is the Gospels, then, of all the Bible, that we should read most often, with most reverence, and with most enjoyment. In this chapter I propose to consider our approach to the first three—those which, written within a few years and having much of their material in common, are known as the Synoptic Gospels. From these three the Fourth Gospel is evidently different in date, in character, and in point of view.

II

Many of us read comparatively seldom in the Gospels from a vague belief that we know them already. Even if that be true, always there is more to be learnt. Perhaps the witness of personal experience may be cited here. At times I have cause to work over some part of the New Testament with special care—collating the Greek texts and their various readings, using the fresh light on the New Testament vocabulary which the papyri have given us, consulting commentaries old and modern, searching the technical journals for expert discussion of particular difficulties ; with the help of this accumulated material the text is studied again, and finally the results are shaped into a lecture or a chapter of a book. But so surely as I imagine then that I really know this part of the New Testament, I open on it casually, or hear it read in church—and on the instant some new parallel, some new felicity, some new shade of meaning leaps, as it were, to light. I feel sure that this experience is common, and that many other students have found in this inexhaustible richness of the Bible that quality which distinguishes it with most clearness from other literature.

Yet we must own that our familiarity with the Gospels is very apt to make us read them with less than full attention, and therefore with less than full enjoyment. Perhaps the most direct means of mastering this danger is to place ourselves in imagination among the people who listened to the words of Christ. It is not the scenery and setting that matter, but the religion and ideas of the folk among whom Christ lived. If in any measure we can realize these, at once we shall find a new significance in the Gospels. Sayings which nineteen centuries have smoothed into tranquil truisms will regain something of that force which made their first hearers stagger with amazement. They believed that the one virtue was " righteousness," that this righteousness began and ended with observance of the vastly intricate Rabbinical code, that the Pharisees and their scribes alone came near to this standard. Then a Rabbi, as they accounted him, declared that they could not enter God's kingdom unless their righteousness exceeded the righteousness of the Pharisees ! His whole doctrine was bewilderingly novel; His view of God, His estimates of moral right and wrong, His judgments of conduct and motive, challenged beliefs which all others of their religious leaders thought fundamental. *" What is this ? A new teaching ! "* cried astonished multitudes. I must not try here to fill in the details of the picture. But I am sure that the story of the Gospels has a new fascination when we remind ourselves of the conditions in which Christ spoke His message; when, having understood more clearly the difficulties of His task, we watch His methods in fulfilling it.

To this suggestion let another be added. If we are rightly to enjoy the Gospels, we should read them with eye and ear alert to notice their charm of detail. We must not turn a page carelessly because, in the main, its contents are familiar and its lessons understood. This they may be; yet it will be strange if we have not missed lesser points which, when observed, must stir our admiring wonder—admiration of their beauty, wonder that we left them so long unregarded. For example, most of us will suppose that we know the parables exceedingly well. They were put before us in our childhood. We have heard them expounded in countless sermons. Phrases and imagery from them have become part of our language. Yet this long acquaintance may be the very cause why many of us have never quite realized their full marvel. These are the finest short stories in the world. Their construction, their rigid economy of material sketching a vivid portrait in a sentence, the exactly right proportion with which subordinate detail is kept in its place yet contributes to the whole effect, their notes, varying with the theme, of warning, irony, tender appeal—such are a few of the qualities which make our Lord's parables unique in literature. Nor, on occasion, was humour lacking from them. When that unforgettable picture was given of the man with a beam in his eye plunging after his neighbour and saying " let me pull out the mote out of thine eye "—then surely a wave of laughter swept over the listening crowd.

It has been said often that the miracles were acted parables. With at least an equal truth we may add that the parables were spoken miracles. The more closely we examine them, the more overwhelming will their perfection seem. Readers have been apt to suppose—without, probably, giving the matter much thought—that these surpassing stories were happy improvisations of the moment. It seems incredible, anyhow, that the longer parables—things exquisitely perfect in every detail, as the stories of the Good Samaritan and of the Prodigal Son—could have been suddenly extemporized. Rather I like to think that here we may find what will be to most of us, perhaps, a new aspect of our Lord's life on earth. He prepared His teaching carefully. This was one use to which He turned those hours spent apart. Work of this quality was not achieved without effort. He knew the difficulties and the joys of creative art as He gave Himself to fashioning these matchless parables. All of us who write, or indeed practise any art, may find help in that thought.

III

Here is one of the shortest parables :

The ground of a certain rich man brought forth plentifully. And he thought within himself, saying, What shall I do, because I have no room where to bestow my fruits ? And he said, This will I do : I will pull down my barns, and build greater ; and there will I bestow all my fruits and my goods. And I will say to my soul, Soul, thou hast much goods laid up for many years ; take thine ease, eat, drink, and be merry. But God said

60

unto him, Thou fool, this night thy soul shall be required of thee : then whose shall those things be, which thou hast provided ?

None can miss, and comment were vain to emphasize, that solemnity of warning. But was ever before or since the tragedy of a life set forth like this in a hundred words? We see it all; we know the man, watch him revelling in his un-earned prosperity, catch the very tone of his sensuous complacency as he plans his future; there falls the lightning-stroke of the catastrophe, the awful scorn in the divine summons : why, many a skilled writer would need a volume for the development of that story, and then would fail to give it the force compressed here into five sentences.

Thus if we are fully to enjoy the Synoptic Gospels, we are not to pass swiftly over the parables, which make up so large a share of their contents. (In striking contrast, the Fourth Gospel has no parables at all.) However well we suppose ourselves to know them, we should taste their beauty afresh, and look for points that escaped us before. Rarely shall we look in vain. Perhaps this counsel can be made more clear by taking one example, and applying to it the kind of method which elsewhere the reader might try for himself. For the purpose let us take that which of all is probably the most familiar—the parable of the Prodigal Son. I need not reprint its text at length, but will note points here and there.

"*A certain man had two sons, and the younger said to his father, Father, give me the portion of goods that falleth to me.*" We must not think this request strange or unfilial. It was a common practice for parents in old age to anticipate (as we should say) their testamentary dispositions, and while still alive to divide their inheritance among their children. (Not a few people, with an eye to death-duties, take this step in our own days.) Jewish law recognized the practice, making the support of the parents thereafter a legal charge upon the children. And we shall remember how Christ denounced those who evaded the obligation, under pretence that all their goods were " corban," had been transferred to the priests for sacred use.

So the younger son takes his journey into a far country. Why did he leave home? Partly, perhaps, because a jealous elder brother had made the home intolerable for him. The Teller of the parable knew all about that, had been driven from His own home by brethren who mocked Him and derided His claims. Follows the story of " the rake's progress "; nowhere else in all literature drawn with touches so few yet so sure and poignant. No long abstract descriptions of penury could match that concrete picture of the swineherd who would fain have filled his belly with the husks that the swine did eat. Presently *" he came to himself."* The comfort of that word ! This is how our Lord views sin ; as something extrinsic to man, foreign to his real nature, a fit of madness which possesses him. When he turns to goodness he does not, as we say, " become another man "; he " comes to himself."

The Prodigal resolves to go back. Will his father receive him ? He makes up beforehand— how true to life !—the sentence he means to speak. But the father is watching, as he has watched through weary days, for his coming. *" When he was yet a great way off, his father saw him, and had compassion, and ran "* (an old man, but now he needs must run !) *" and fell on his neck and kissed him."* The son begins the sentence he has prepared : *" Father, I have sinned against heaven and in thy sight, and am no more worthy to be called thy son "*—and stops abruptly. *" Make me as one of thy hired servants ! "* he had planned to add. But he cannot. It had seemed a fit enough request when he was far away. It is impossible as he stands now, face to face with

63

his father, knowing what sonship will mean. Not easily, I think, can you match that touch— the piercing truth and insight shown by leaving that sentence unfinished.

Then the feast of welcome is spread, and we pass to the sequel. (Reflect again on the impossibility of supposing all this tale, with its perfect construction, to have been devised on the spur of the moment.) We seem to catch the very tone of the aggrieved elder son, unmoved by the pathos of his father's entreaty : " *Lo, these many years do I serve thee, neither transgressed I at any time thy commandment ; but thou never gavest me a kid* "—much less the fatted calf—" *that I might make merry with my friends.*" (Significant pronouns ! He would not have had his father present.) " *But as soon as this thy son was come* " (not *my brother*, but *thy son*; " this precious son of thine ") " *thou hast killed for him the fatted calf.*"

And then the reply, bringing the tale to its glorious close : " *Son, thou art ever with me, and all that I have is thine. It was meet that we should make merry, and be glad ; for this thy brother* " (not " my son " only; how tender the rebuke !) " *was dead and is alive again ; and was lost, and is found.*"

We do not lessen the divine comfort of that

saying when we observe the art with which our
English translators have wrought its exquisite
cadence : the gradual broadening of the vowels—
" *dead*," " *alive*," " *lost*," " *found*," that last full,
strong note closing nobly the whole; and, again,
the ascent, as it were, narrowing evenly to the
summit; six syllables answering six, then three
answering three; " this thy brother was dead ";
" and is alive again "; " and was lost "; " and
is found."

If the reader had noticed already every detail
of the parable emphasized here, even then he
will not resent, I think, this attempt to illustrate
observant reading by a definite example. Such
reading is possible for all of us. It is not suggested to replace either devotional meditation or
exact study. But if it helps us, as I am sure it
can help, to read the Gospels with a keener enjoyment, it will not fail to profit both spirit and
mind.

IV

A book of this kind cannot try to deal fully
with all the intricacies of the " Synoptic problem,"
or with the many points of higher criticism which
are, and seem likely to remain, in dispute. As,

however, the greater part are of minor and technical interest, they need not have place in pages written to increase enjoyment of the Bible rather than argument about it. But, distinct from these subsidiary problems, the main results of modern criticism—the results which to-day virtually all scholars accept—do aid enjoyment. They answer questions which must occur to every thoughtful reader of the Synoptic Gospels.

Thus he will have observed that some incidents are recorded by one Gospel alone, others by two or all three. Further, he will have seen that sometimes the accounts in two or three Gospels correspond so closely in their wording that they cannot have been written independently. Then again, in the midst of this verbal identity he may light on a sudden and significant change of phrase, where obviously one evangelist has altered, of set purpose, the language of another. Naturally the reader will ask how these facts are to be interpreted, and it is here that the established results of criticism will help him. Briefly, they are as follows.

Mark is the earliest of the three Synoptic Gospels. Whether Matthew was written before or after Luke is uncertain, and, relatively, unimportant. The memorable point is that the writers of Matthew and Luke had Mark before them as they worked. It has been calculated that of the six hundred and sixty verses composing Mark, Matthew and Luke have used between them no fewer than six hundred and ten. These two writers seem also to have utilized another early document, surviving only in the quotations they make from it. This may have been a collection of sayings spoken by our Lord rather than a continuous record of His ministry. Thus the materials used by Matthew and Luke would be (*a*) Mark; (*b*) the lost document; (*c*) independent information collected separately by each writer.

St. Mark, the author of the oldest Gospel we possess, is said by an ancient tradition to have derived his information about our Lord's ministry from St. Peter, and a good deal of indirect evidence may be found in Mark to support this view. Many commentators suggest that the " certain young man " who followed Jesus in Gethsemane and fled naked from those who tried to seize him was St. Mark himself. The case for this theory is, I think, very strong indeed on literary grounds. There is no mention of the incident in any of the other Gospels. If it describes a personal experience of the author, its introduction is entirely natural. Otherwise there seems no reason for it. This was not merely " a young man " but " a certain young man "—*i.e.*, one whom the writer could name if he chose. And if St. Mark was in Jerusalem through the week immediately before the Passion and could describe its events as an eye-witness, we can understand why the record of this one week forms nearly a third part of the whole Gospel.

The reader should note that Mark breaks off abruptly at ch. xvi. 8. The original ending may have been lost, or St. Mark's work may have been interrupted by illness, imprisonment, or death. The remaining verses of the chapter that are printed in our Bible were added by a later hand. An alternative and shorter ending also was known in early days. It is important for us to remember that we cannot rightly quote or argue from *vv.* 9–20 as if they formed part of the Gospel, for they do not.

In reading Mark we should notice specially the bustling vividness of the style—the word rendered " straightway " or " immediately " is one of St. Mark's favourites; the fact that, in comparison with the other Synoptic Gospels, more space is given for our Lord's deeds and less to His words; and the simple candour with which the completeness of His humanity is recognized. Yet Mark gives no countenance to those who argue that Jesus did not claim divinity for Himself, and that this was a belief of gradual development among His followers. Not from the latest, but from this, the earliest, of our Gospels we take the record :

Again the high priest asked him, and said unto him, Art thou the Christ, the Son of the Blessed ? And Jesus said, I am.

In all this Gospel there is nothing to match the importance of that " I am."

We do not know who wrote—or, to use a more accurate word, compiled—Matthew in its present shape. An ancient witness states that St. Matthew made in Aramaic a collection of our Lord's sayings. It seems possible that parts of this, translated into Greek, were incorporated in Matthew and gave it its name. But that St. Matthew is in any further sense the author of this Gospel seems most unlikely. He was one of the Twelve. He accompanied our Lord throughout His ministry. Therefore it seems incredible that he would have borrowed Mark's account of it, as the author of Matthew did, in place of describing in his own words the events of which he himself had been an eye-witness. The reader should notice how the writer of Matthew was perturbed by Mark's frankness, fearing that it would cause misunderstandings. Therefore he strikes out phrases which show the disciples in an unfavourable light, and those which emphasize Christ's humanity—such as the statements that He " sighed " and " marvelled "; while " Why callest thou Me good ? " is transformed by Matthew into " Why askest thou Me concerning that which is good ? "

As Mark was the earliest of the Gospels, we might have expected it to be placed first in order when the four were brought together. But Matthew was given this position doubtless because it served peculiarly well to link the Old Testament with the New. It was written for Jewish readers, and therefore abounds with references to their Scriptures. St. Mark, writing for Gentiles, wishes simply to relate the story of our Lord's work. Quotations from the Old Testament would have no interest for his readers. But the writer of Matthew feels that his chief aim must be to prove that Jesus was the Messiah whom the Jews expected, and that His life and words " fulfilled " exactly the Old Testament Scriptures. To remember the dominance of this special aim is the key to a right understanding of Matthew, and most of all when we compare it with the other Synoptic Gospels.

The pages in it to which the general reader turns most often are, beyond doubt, those of the fifth, sixth, and seventh chapters. The Sermon on the Mount sets forth, with matchless clarity, the ideals of Christian character. Its insight, its nobility, its range of vision have compelled the wonder of mankind. Because the Jews had looked for a divinely ordered kingdom to free them from alien thrall, Matthew puts in the forefront all that Jesus taught of the kingdom of Heaven. And the Sermon on the Mount describes the character which one desiring citizenship in that kingdom must strive to attain.

To-day, however, nearly all technical experts agree that the contents of these three chapters are not one connected discourse but a selection from many. According to this view, Matthew's "Sermon on the Mount" is made up of (a) the briefer "Sermon on the Plain" recorded by St. Luke, and (b) detached sayings of Christ, spoken at various times, and grouped here as a convenient summary of His doctrine. But this question is of a kind, I suggest, on which an academic judgment need not be taken as final. The general reader, if he be equipped with the literary sense, has a right to be heard, for literary sense perceives evidence to which merely technical learning is apt to be blind. No doubt Luke's sermon, like Matthew's, opens with the beatitudes—though strikingly varied—and some of the teaching that follows is common to both. Yet how odd is the assumption that our Lord would not repeat to different audiences the same teaching! What is the accustomed method of those who have to instruct or persuade listening crowds in many places? Certainly to reiterate the truths that seem of highest importance, and, finding in one place that some illustration or anecdote is specially effective, to use it again elsewhere. Possibly, though, they will change the wording, or add details that will appeal to the particular audience of the moment. Yet no teacher, and least of all an itinerant teacher, would shrink from repeating himself. I believe that the disciples probably heard most of the parables many times over, which explains in part why they were remembered with such exactness. And it seems mere pedantry to argue that because our Lord spoke the beatitudes in the Sermon on the Plain, recorded by Luke, He could not have spoken them also in that other Sermon on the Mount which Matthew describes.

There is a further test which we may find it of interest to apply for ourselves. Let the reader go rapidly through the whole Sermon on the Mount in Matthew. Then let him ask what impression it has made on him. While claiming no finality for my judgment, I can only say that I can find in it no reason for doubting Matthew's explicit statement that the whole was delivered at one time in the setting he describes. At one point I hesitate; the text of the Lord's Prayer does not seem quite in place, and I think that possibly enough Matthew introduced it here as a kind of footnote to the teaching about prayer. For the rest, however, the Sermon seems a carefully constructed whole, the points of which follow in an orderly sequence, until the splendid and dramatic parable is reached which forms the fitting end. The Sermon does not read to me in the least like an anthology of detached sayings and fragments of teaching compiled by the writer of the Gospel. Other readers may find themselves driven to the opposite opinion. What chiefly I wish to urge is that they should make this very interesting experiment for themselves, and form their own judgments. They need not bow to the verdict of the critics. For this is one of the questions to which I have referred already—questions on which the general reader, if he have the literary instinct, is more qualified to decide than any academic professor of Hellenistic Greek.

St. Luke introduces his Gospel with a most carefully written preface, modelled after an ancient pattern—much as if to-day a writer prefixed to his work an " epistle dedicatory " written in the style of the eighteenth century. We may notice that he was moved to write his Gospel by the example of many others, whose books have not survived. " Forasmuch as many," he begins; ". . . it seemed good to me also "—this is not the phrasing we might have expected. A modern author would have written " although " in place of " forasmuch as." " Although many valuable works on this subject are already in existence, yet I have ventured " . . . we are familiar with that note in a preface. But the fact that so many others have written Gospels is the reason why St. Luke has taken courage to write his. Not vain, then, was the toil of these nameless and forgotten writers ! If their own books perished quickly, indirectly they brought into being one to enrich mankind through all time. But for these forgotten Gospels, we should have had no Gospel of Luke. We should not have had (for no other of the surviving Gospels gives us) those incomparable Christmas scenes of the shepherds, the herald angels, and the manger. We should have had no *Magnificat*. We should have lacked the loveliest of the parables. Indeed, for sheer charm this exceeds, I think, both the other synoptic Gospels.

Of the various sources from which St. Luke gathered his materials, the Gospel of Mark was the chief. He reproduces it with fewer changes than are found in Matthew's transcripts from it, but we should notice some very interesting alterations in his accounts of miracles of healing. Often Mark's description did not satisfy him as a medical man, and he would bring it more into line with the professional knowledge of his day. A late tradition asserts that St. Luke was a painter as well as a physician; certainly the gift of vivid word-painting was his. We may note, too, his obvious sympathy with the poor and contempt of misused wealth. Whether his own feelings on this subject led him unconsciously to put our Lord's words about it in a rather false perspective, is a question not easy to decide. Yet that the Master's view of poverty and wealth as presented in the third Gospel differs from that given in the first and second seems indubitable. And therefore we should be unwise to draw conclusions from either strain of teaching by itself, forgetting the existence of the other.

To read the Synoptic Gospels often and fully and freely is to escape from this and from kindred dangers. We shall not view them as a collection of " texts," a store of independent moral maxims. Instead, we shall take the three books as one great whole, as a magnificent piece of literature, every page of which amplifies and illuminates the rest. We may choose one or another of the three for our favourite, yet the effect of any will be far less than the effect of all. Again and again we shall return to read at large in those pages, so human and so divine, and ever will they stir in us new awe, and admiration, and keen delight.

CHAPTER IV   THE FOURTH GOSPEL

I

With most questions of authorship and date
there is little need to concern ourselves when we
read the Bible for enjoyment. The music of a
Psalm, for instance, is no less exquisite because
another than David wrote it. That glorious
eulogy of faith in the Epistle to the Hebrews
appeals as much to us as to our ancestors, who
attributed it mistakenly to St. Paul. If two—
or, more probably, many—persons contributed to
the writings that bear the name of Isaiah, that is
an interesting piece of knowledge, yet it affects
neither the spiritual nor the literary value of
those great rhapsodies. But when we are to
read the Fourth Gospel, the question of its source
and character needs must be faced. For upon
the answer will depend our whole attitude in
approaching the book. Were the point at issue
merely whether it was St. John the Apostle or
some other eye-witness who set down his memories
in these pages, it would matter comparatively

little. But it does not matter little when many erudite critics assert that the Fourth Gospel has no historic character at all. They suppose that the words and deeds attributed to Christ are, in fact, pious imaginations. Some unknown writer, meditating on the divine nature of our Lord, sought to convey these thoughts to others in a picturesque form. He did not intend it to be taken as history; that need had been met long before by the Synoptic Gospels. He proposed to illustrate our Lord's character, as it were, by picturing things of the kind He might have done and words of the kind He might have said. As little did he mean them to be taken for records of fact as the author of *The Imitation of Christ* meant us to think that the words he attributes to God in those colloquies with the soul came literally from the Divine mouth.

Such, in brief, is the view held by critics of the " extreme " school. If it be demonstrably true, we must accept it, at whatever cost. Yet the critics themselves shrink from the most obvious consequence of acceptance when they speak still of " the Fourth Gospel." If they be right, this book is not a Gospel at all. A Gospel is an authentic record of what Jesus did and taught. This has even become an axiom of common talk, so that people speak of " gospel truth." A

Gospel which is a work of imagination is a contradiction in terms. Here, then, is a question which the general reader is bound to face. For the most part, he may be little disposed to investigate the niceties of biblical criticism, and prefer to leave them to experts. He may feel that the results, one way or another, will not greatly affect his enjoyment of the Bible. But the question raised over this part of the New Testament is not one which even the most casual reader can treat as secondary. Before he sits down to this book he must know, not necessarily its exact date or authorship, but whether he is about to read a Gospel or a work of imagination. In either event it may be beautiful and interesting. Yet the beauty and interest will vary not merely in degree but in kind.

At this stage, therefore, I urge the reader to study this problem of the Fourth Gospel for himself. He need not deem the enterprise beyond his powers. He may lack technical scholarship, yet if he bring to the task a real feeling for literature and a knowledge of human nature, he will be able to apply tests, the value of which is too often ignored. Again, he will be more likely than the expert to begin with an open mind. The theologian clinging yet to the older theories of inspiration will deny that the case presented by the extreme critics deserves any consideration at all. More common to-day is the theologian who has arrived at a form of belief—a Christology —which satisfies himself, but somehow cannot at all be reconciled with the teaching of the Fourth Gospel. Not much evidence is needed to convince him that the Fourth Gospel is unauthentic.

Probably the reader will ask himself at the outset whether it seems likely that a devout disciple in the first century would attempt imaginative work of this kind. Would he invent incidents that never happened and describe our Lord's part in them, add fictitious details to the stories of the Crucifixion and Resurrection? Would he attribute to the Master long discourses every word of which, in fact, was his own? If he did all this, and put such a work into circulation, would he make no effort to ensure that its fictitious character should be understood? When he found that it was being read as literal history, would he leave the readers thus misled? If, again, he did nothing, is it probable that no one else would, and that a work of this nature, so different from the authentic Gospels, would be received unhesitatingly as an historic record, as a genuine Gospel, by the Christian Church? For there is ample evidence that so early as the second century this book was accepted by the Christian community,

not merely as a Gospel, but as a Gospel written
by St. John. And whose mind was it that was
capable of inventing (for example) the discourses
in the Upper Room?

II

Such are some of the questions which, with
many more, will promptly occur to the reader.
Already he will feel that whatever be the obstacles
to hinder acceptance of the traditional view, the
rival theory of the critics is not without difficulties of its own. What, then, he will enquire,
are the reasons why the traditional belief must be
set aside? If through ages reaching back to the
second century this book has been accounted the
Gospel of St. John, why are we driven to hold it
not by St. John and not a Gospel, but an anony-
mous romance, which gained a place in the Bible
under false pretences?

For many reasons, reply the critics. And chief
among them is the immense and patent contrast
between the Fourth Gospel and the earlier three.
It is not merely that there are discrepancies of
detail, though some of these are grave. It is not
merely that the Fourth Gospel omits events of a
chief importance in our Lord's life and includes

others so striking that (thus runs the argument) the synoptists could not have known them and have left them unmentioned. More significant than any such points is the vital difference between the Christ presented by the first three Gospels and the Christ presented by the fourth. In the former His human nature is emphasized, and He expounds with homely illustrations the kind of life His disciples ought to live in this world. In the latter He is concerned to teach theological truth, and to set forth his mystical union with the Father. And the Fourth Gospel is so phrased that often we are left unsure at what point the words attributed to Christ cease and the writer's exposition of them begins. But this Gospel was written at a date close to the year 90. Is it credible that anyone would be able then to write from memory long discourses that had been spoken sixty years before? If we maintain that St. John wrote it, and assume that he was but a youth of twenty when he walked with our Lord, he would be eighty when he made this Gospel. And against the tradition that he lived to extreme old age in Ephesus must be set another, that he perished many years earlier as a martyr.

Such, in outline, is the critics' argument. The reader may feel that it scarcely disposes of the difficulties that already have occurred to him, and, in particular, that it does not explain how a book of this kind came to be accepted at once as the authentic Gospel of St. John. And there are further points, not to be neglected because they are untechnical, and even rather obvious. For instance, is it really surprising that this Gospel should differ from the others in character and treatment? No evangelist could hope to deal completely with his theme. Mark described our Lord's life and work from a special point of view, which guided his choice of incidents. As Matthew and Luke were based on Mark, they followed the same general lines. When a Fourth Gospel was to be written, would not its author naturally choose other events to describe? However important some episode might be, it would appear futile to narrate once more what all his readers knew quite well already. Again, if the first three Gospels had emphasized the perfect humanity of our Lord, might we not expect the writer of the Fourth to make his work the complement of theirs, and to lay stress upon Christ's divinity? Indeed, that this was the aim of the writer of the Fourth Gospel we know from his own words. Looking back upon his pages as he comes to their end, he says : " *These are written that ye might believe that Jesus is the Christ, the*

Son of God." That seems an inept argument which tries to discredit the Fourth Gospel because it does not repeat what already is familiar, and because its character differs from the Marcan tradition embodied in the other three.

Once more, when the reader turns to the evidence of the book itself, he is freed from a confusion of thought which is strangely frequent even in learned treatises. Having fixed the " date " of this Gospel at about A.D. 90, they assume that this was, approximately, the time when it was written, and base their principal arguments on this assumption. But were the critics as well versed in the methods of literary craftsmanship as they are in technical learning they would not build their case on so slight a foundation. When we say that the year 90 was the " date " of the Fourth Gospel, we mean no more than that this was the time when the Gospel, in the shape we now have, was first put into circulation. It might have been written much earlier. And when we examine it, we learn from its own statement that it was brought to its present form by two stages, and by two people. First, a disciple wrote an account of what he had seen and heard as he accompanied the Master. Afterwards someone else gathered together these writings, probably made a selection from them, and arranged them as the Gospel given to the Church in the year 90. The author wrote anonymously, and the editor does not disclose his name, but identifies him with " the disciple whom Jesus loved." " *This*," he says in an editorial note, " *is the disciple which testifieth of these things and wrote these things ; and we know that his testimony is true.*" If, then, the critics are right in believing this book to be a work of imagination, we are to suppose that the actual writer invented an author, described in this curious way as " the disciple whom Jesus loved "; invented an editor, and made the imaginary editor testify, in this solemn fashion, to the truth of the imaginary tale of the imaginary author. That does not seem very plausible. It does not seem likely that a devout Christian would have clothed his own meditations, by this elaborate means, in the form of a Gospel. It does not seem likely that, had he done so, his work would have been accepted by the Church as a genuine Gospel.

On the other hand, let us assume for the moment that the material of the book is drawn from the written recollections of the beloved disciple, as the editor states. Let us assume also that the beloved disciple was St. John—and indeed it is most difficult to identify him with anyone else. Then we have no need to suppose that St.

John waited until some sixty years after our Lord's ministry to set down his account of it. A volume of reminiscences is published in 1925. In that sense, 1925 is its "date." Yet the chances are that its contents come from diaries, letters, and descriptions written many years earlier. I think the reader of the Fourth Gospel will feel that its narratives were written quite soon after the happening of the events they describe. That would explain how the small details of a scene can be given, how the Master's words can be recorded at length.

I am almost inclined to believe that St. John began by trying to keep a day-by-day diary. After the introduction in chapter i we have the story of the first day. Then, at verse 29, we pass to "on the morrow"; in verse 35, again "on the morrow"; in verse 43 "on the morrow," and the extract—or the diary itself—ends after the beginning of chapter ii, "on the third day." But almost all the narratives sound as if they describe what is still fresh in the writer's memory. Read again, for example, the story of the wedding at Cana. It abounds with vivid and unexpected details, such as no one writing a fictitious story would have imagined; details which seem to argue that here is an account by a very observant eye-witness. Or consider the fourteenth, fifteenth, and sixteenth chapters.   In all the Bible there are perhaps none more beautiful, none to which burdened souls in every age have turned more often for strength and consolation. *" Peace I leave with you ; my peace I give unto you ; not as the world giveth, give I unto you.   Let not your heart be troubled, neither let it be afraid."   " In my Father's house are many mansions : if it were not so, I would have told you.   I go to prepare a place for you."   " In the world ye shall have tribulation ; but be of good cheer ; I have overcome the world."* The cadence of those words haunts us like beautiful music.   The message of the chapters makes them a spiritual treasure; the perfection of their wording sets them among the supreme things in literature.   Various parts of the New Testament appeal in varying degrees to various readers, but probably there have been no readers who would not name this Discourse in the Upper Room as the pages which brought them most of happiness.

III

Yet our joy in them will not silence the question how they came into our possession.   In ages less critical it sufficed people to believe, without enquiry, that Jesus spoke these words and that St.

John wrote them down. For my own part, I hold this to be true. But at one important point it is no longer possible for us to share the faith of our ancestors. Had they been asked how St. John at the age of eighty could record with verbal exactness this long discourse, to which (with a very dim apprehension of its meaning) he had listened as a youth of twenty, they would have been content to answer that St. John was divinely inspired, and so was enabled supernaturally to reproduce the precise words spoken in the Upper Room, beyond possibility of error. Even now this theory of verbal inspiration lingers among simple souls, whose content with it none should willingly disturb. But it is impossible for any who are able to bring modern knowledge to their reading of the New Testament. When it is evident beyond doubt, for instance, that Matthew and Luke deliberately altered as they copied the words of Mark—Matthew because some of Mark's phrases seemed dangerous, Luke because his medical knowledge suggested amendment—the idea that Matthew, Mark, and Luke alike were written down automatically, as it were, at the dictation of the Holy Spirit, is an idea that must be abandoned. Then, however, we have to own the difficulty of supposing that after an interval of sixty years anyone could reproduce the lengthy teaching in the Upper Room word for word as it had been spoken by the Master. This may not be impossible, but it does seem most unlikely.

Yet I think that anyone of literary sense would be driven to believe this happened rather than accept the explanation which the extreme critics offer :—the explanation that the whole of this book is simply the romance of a pious idealist, that the Upper Room discourses, like all the other chapters, are mere fiction. Here the very men who are anxious to remove " the miraculous element " from the Gospel narratives are making one of the Gospels itself a miracle which does indeed stagger belief. Let the reader test this for himself. Let him go through the Fourth Gospel afresh. Let him inhibit by a conscious act of the will, so far as he may, all previous memories of it. Let him try to gain the impression it would make on him were he opening it for the first time. Let him read it with all the literary sensitiveness he can command. And, as he closes the book at the end, let him consider once more what it is that the academic critics ask him to believe : that some nameless and quite unknown Jew of the first century invented the character of Christ as shown in this book, invented the " beloved disciple " as its author, invented an editor to collect the writings of the beloved disciple and to append footnotes, invented the characters of the other disciples and of the scores of people described with convincing touches in these pages, invented every minute detail of the incidents recorded— details of a most unexpected kind—invented the teaching ascribed to Christ, with its matchless beauty, tenderness, surprise, serene wisdom, knowledge of human nature—invented, from first to last, the scenes and the discourses in the Upper Room, invented details about what was to him the death of the Son of God, invented the garden-scene of the Resurrection, and that other scene by the lake. . . . I need not prolong the list. Let the reader use his own judgment. He may be able to accept this theory of the Fourth Gospel's origin. Personally, I cannot. And, so far as I can tell, it is not any theological bias, but all that I know of literature and human limitations which compels me to reject this view, no matter by how erudite a scholasticism it be supported. That phrase must not be taken to imply that all the critical experts are on one side. Of late there has been a reaction among them; far more incline now to accept the Fourth Gospel as, in the main, an authentic work of historic value. And this is the question we have to settle. Whether the eye-witness who wrote it was St. John the Apostle or some other, whether or no a number of editorial notes were incorporated in his work, are points that matter comparatively little. But in order to enjoy this book rightly, we must make up our minds whether it is a record of fact or a pious romance.

Let us return for a moment to the Upper Room discourses. If we cannot accept either the theory of verbal inspiration or that of the extreme critics, is any other explanation at hand to help us? There is; one which seems to be both simple and satisfying. It supposes that St. John committed them to writing, not sixty years, but twenty-four hours, after they were spoken, while their words were fresh in his memory; that he recalled them on the night after the Crucifixion, for the comfort of the Lord's Mother, who had been committed to his care.[1]

Long years afterwards, this document, together with others in which the disciple had recorded the things he had heard and seen, were shaped by an editor into the book we now possess. This editor felt that they should be made known to the Church, and that they would be of special profit at a time when many had begun to be doubtful of our Lord's divinity. This Gospel, he

[1] Obviously, this is no more than a conjecture, but one for which, I believe, there is much to be said. I have discussed it more fully elsewhere.—See *Rabboni*, ch. iv. (Hodder & Stoughton.)

saw, would complete as well as confirm the work already done by the earlier three. From the beloved disciple's records he chose, so far as he could, those incidents which had not been described already. To use all the material was impossible. He laments this humorously in his final footnote, with its reference to " the many other things " which Jesus did, "*the which, if they should be written every one, I suppose that even the world itself could not contain the books that should be written.*"

Does the reader feel that this chapter is rather foreign to the title and avowed purpose of my volume? Really it is not. In other chapters there will be no need to discuss matters of biblical criticism at any length. But in this respect the Fourth Gospel stands apart. As I have urged, we must decide for ourselves its essential character before we can obtain full enjoyment from it. Yet this close examination with a special end in view will itself be found pleasurable. At least it will profit the reader, and not himself alone, no matter to what opinion it lead him. Scholastic criticism, for all its high value, is apt to claim an infallibility it does not possess, and to suggest that its decisions must be accepted meekly by the general reader. Yet it needs to be supplemented and corrected by readers who, if unversed in the Hellenistic use of the aorist and such-like matters, do know some-thing of, and perhaps themselves have practised, the art of literature. And this special problem of the Fourth Gospel is not one that we can afford to leave unsolved. It is not an academic matter, but one of the most direct practical importance. For to-day we are challenged imperatively by the question, " What think ye of Christ? " And, in a very large degree, our answer to that question must be shaped by what we think of the Fourth Gospel.

I

THE Acts of the Apostles is probably the last book of the New Testament to which the average reader would turn with hopes of enjoyment. His memory is weighted against it. It recalls some of the bleakest hours of his schooldays, when he must journey unwillingly with St. Paul, beware of confusing Antioch in Syria with Antioch in Pisidia, and memorize the routes of this indefatigable traveller. Scripture lessons have been improved since those days, but in the past one of their most lamentable results was an enduring distaste for this part of the Scriptures. It is well worth while to overcome that prejudice. In point of fact we shall find, examining the book with maturer judgment, that it is precisely the chapters we disliked most—those which describe St. Paul's missionary journeys—that compel our fullest admiration. We may admit that the Acts is a very unequal book. St. Luke seems to have been far less interested in St. Peter than in

94

St. Paul. The earlier chapters have their fine moments, but, as a whole, are written in a flat and perfunctory fashion. With the appearance of Saul of Tarsus the tone changes. The writing begins to glow. Unimportant details and episodes are summarized in a few sentences, so that they may not weaken the effect of the great scenes. These are set forth fully, with wonderful dramatic force; they are, indeed, triumphs of literary craftsmanship. No other New Testament writer, except that unknown genius who wrote Hebrews, can match St. Luke in culture or technical skill. And this book gives him fuller scope than his Gospel for the use of his powers. In the Gospel there was far less of his own writing. Through a large part of it, as we have seen, he was transcribing and amending Mark; also, like Matthew, he borrowed much from that collection of our Lord's sayings which in its original form has disappeared. But the Acts is his own book throughout, and in describing St. Paul's journeys he tells often (as the use of the pronoun " we " reveals) of adventures which he himself has shared.

With his picturesqueness he unites a power of close observation and extreme accuracy in detail. For instance, he terms the local magistrates at Thessalonica " politarchs." This is a rare word, unknown to classical literature. Hostile critics were in the habit of citing its use to discredit St. Luke's truthfulness. And then in the last century a Roman arch was discovered at Saloniki itself with the word " politarch " upon it. Again, the busy idlers of Athens used a word of Attic slang when they derided St. Paul. They called him, not a " babbler," as our version renders it, but " a seed-picker "—a collector, that is, of scraps of knowledge. St. Luke's ear noted the slang word, and it was set down in his story. More famous, of course, is his account of the shipwreck. This is gallantly done, with a fine sureness of touch. And sailors testify that every point of seamanship in it is right. I think that St. Luke loved the sea. In his land-journeys not once does he name any incident of the road; he is content to say merely that " we departed from " this place, " and came to " that. But he will have us know each detail of a voyage. When his ship has made an unusually quick passage from Troas to Neapolis, this is a fact which he must note. In all the later parts of the Acts, too, we shall find pleasure in the extraordinarily deft sketches of the minor characters. Almost any page will give examples. Consider, for one, the story of the Ephesian riot, and the inimitable speech of Demetrius, silversmith, to " the workers of like occupation," protesting vehemently that through St. Paul's influence their craft ("by which we have our wealth") will be endangered, and then adding, as a lesser thing, that it will also dishonour the goddess of the city. And the town-clerk's speech which follows has the very ring of perturbed officialdom. The whole story lives.

II

Perhaps the one disappointment of this book is the manner of its ending. That, at a first sight, does seem strangely abrupt and unsatisfying. We feel that we are about to reach what should be the finest and most important scenes of all. St. Paul, the Roman citizen, has arrived in Rome, where he is to plead before Cæsar. But nothing follows beyond a two-verse summary of two years. We are told that St. Paul dwelt through that time in "his own hired house," received visitors, and preached the Gospel, "no man forbidding him." And these are the last words of the book. We feel that it is not finished, but suddenly broken off. The consummate artistry shown by the later chapters makes us marvel that St. Luke should have been content with a conclusion that seems so lame. Is there an explanation? Are we to suppose that the closing pages of this book have been lost, like the original ending of Mark?

One explanation there is which, if true, not only clears this special point, but illuminates the whole of Luke and the Acts. We need not take it as more than a theory. Some of the commentaries do not so much as mention it. Personally, I find it convincing. But, whether or no the reader come to this belief, I am sure that he will find enjoyment in testing it, in keeping this theory before him as he looks through the Acts and observes the evidence to be found for its support.

We may begin with what seems more than a mere conjecture. When Theophilus had read the preface to the Acts he would expect this book to have a sequel, because St. Luke refers to his Gospel not as his " former," but as his " first " treatise. (Our English translators changed the word to " former " to suit the fact that we have but two; the accurate meaning " first " is given in the margin of the Revised Version.) The Greek words for " former " (*i.e.* the prior of two things) and " first " (the earliest of more than two) are different. The distinction was ignored in the ordinary colloquial Greek of the New Testament, as it is in colloquial English. But St. Luke's prefaces are written in fastidiously correct Greek. Therefore we may be sure that he would have mentioned the Gospel as his " former," not as his " first," work had he intended the Acts, his second

98

volume, to be also his last.   We have good reason, then, for saying that he proposed to write a trilogy, of which the first part was his Gospel ; the second was the Acts ; the third was never written—unless it has been lost.

What was that third volume to contain ?   Again we can be reasonably confident about the answer. It would continue the narrative from the stage reached in the last chapter of the Acts.   Volume II had told us how St. Paul appealed from the local to the imperial court, and therefore had been sent to Rome.   Volume III naturally would narrate his first trial there and his acquittal.[1] And, told with all the graphic power of St. Luke, what magnificent reading that would have been !

Thus we come to another question.   St. Luke's primary motive was the historian's.   He wished, as he said himself, to set down facts " accurately

---

[1] Many critics believe St. Paul's martyrdom to have followed immediately his first trial in Rome.   Others (rightly, as I think) support the traditional view, which seems to find support in Clement of Rome, the Muratorian Fragment, and 2 Timothy.   According to this view, St. Paul's expectation of acquittal, shown in his letter to the Philippians, was fulfilled.   He was released and made further missionary journeys—perhaps to Spain— before being again arrested, tried in Rome, and put to death.   Here, as elsewhere in this book, I have to leave an intricate and technical question of evidence undis- cussed, merely assuming the conclusion which seems to me more probably right.

and in order." But had he any more special motive? Was there a reason which led him to cast his work in this particular form? He wrote at a time when the chief danger menacing the Church was the enmity of the Roman Government. Always it viewed the Christians with suspicion, and at times suspicion blazed up into ruthless persecution. Yet this attitude came in part from a misunderstanding.[1] The Church's enemies were eager to assert that the friends of Christ had been identified from the beginning with the enemies of Cæsar. If therefore St. Luke could so write his history as to refute this slander, he might serve the Church in a very effective way. He might persuade the Roman officials, and Cæsar himself, to tolerate Christianity, instead of trying mercilessly to suppress it. And he could hope to do this best not by argument, but by the relation of facts. He would show that the current stories about the early hostility of Rome to the Church were false. When he described St. Paul's work, he would make it plain that, fierce as were the attacks on the Apostle, they came from his own countrymen, the Jews, and not from Rome. He would emphasize the occasions when Roman officials recognized the innocence of the Christians,

[1] Until the cult of emperor-worship made a definite breach with the Church inevitable.

and intervened to save them from the fury of a mob. In short, he would hope to prove that if Cæsar now should countenance persecution, he would be reversing, instead of continuing, the deliberate verdict of official Rome in the past.

Such, then, is the theory of the special purpose with which St. Luke wrote. I suggest that the reader will enjoy the writings with a new zest if he keeps in mind this theory, and observes closely the very numerous points that seem to tell in its favour. Here I can cite but a few of them. In his Gospel St. Luke is at pains, beyond any other evangelist, to show how often and how strongly the Procurator of Judæa declared he could find no fault in the Prisoner haled before him by the Jews. In his second volume he draws, in effective contrast, the portrait of another Roman magistrate, strong as Pilate was weak. Gallio personifies nobly the ideal sung long before by Horace, is the " upright man of fixed purposes, not to be swayed by the base clamour of a mob." And St. Luke records how each Roman court—of Gallio, of Felix, of Festus—asserted, in effect, St. Paul's innocence. He is careful to mention that one Roman official after another, from Sergius Paulus to the governor of Malta, treated the Apostle with approving courtesy. He notes that if Christianity compelled St. Paul to resign his high place among the religious leaders of the Jews, it was not inconsistent, to his thinking, with a full use of Roman citizenship, the privileges of which he was proud still to claim.

And let the reader observe how St. Luke seems to concentrate on his special purpose as he nears the end of the Acts. The trial before Felix is reported at length. Then two years' events are condensed into a single verse. But after this, two complete chapters are devoted to the interviews between St. Paul and Festus. St. Paul refuses to stand for trial before the Jewish council, even though Festus be joined with it as assessor. His words are magnificent :

I stand at Cæsar's judgment seat, where I ought to be judged : to the Jews have I done no wrong, as thou very well knowest. For if I be an offender, or have committed any thing worthy of death, I refuse not to die. But if there be none of these things whereof these Jews accuse me, no man may hand me over as a bribe to them. I appeal unto Cæsar.

A little later, Festus tells Agrippa how the Jews clamoured for instant judgment upon St. Paul, and the very ring of imperial Rome is in his scornful words :

To whom I answered, It is not the manner of the Romans to deliver any man to die before that he which is accused have the accusers face to face, and have licence to answer for himself concerning the crimes laid against him.

All the scene in which St. Paul stands before Festus, Agrippa, and Bernice is superbly told. The Greek style is far more ornate than St. Luke permits himself elsewhere. We are made to see each detail; the court pageant, as the procession enters " with great pomp," the effect of St. Paul's words on the perturbed Agrippa. St. Luke uses all his powers in this chapter, feeling it to be the climax of the Acts. And throughout it the truth he would have understood is made more clear— that St. Paul was sent to Rome not as a con- demned prisoner, but by his own choice. " *This man might have been set at liberty, if he had not appealed unto Cæsar.*"

After this there is but the voyage and the arrival at Rome to be chronicled, and the book is done. How St. Paul fared when at last he stood before Cæsar was to be the theme of a third volume. Alas ! It seems too likely that the recurrence of persecution which the writer had laboured to avert did break out, and that, with his work unfinished, he himself died among its victims.

Yet, before we part from him, let us look again, in the light of the theory we are pondering, at that last sentence of the Acts :

And Paul dwelt two whole years in his own hired house, and received all that came in unto him, preaching the kingdom of God, and teaching those things which concern the Lord Jesus Christ, with all confidence, no man forbidding him.

When first we read it, that seemed a curiously lame and inept ending for a masterpiece of literature. But as we consider it afresh, mindful of the purpose we are supposing St. Luke to have had at heart, does not its high significance dawn on us? These are no casual words, unfit for their place. They drive home their plea. They prove that in the early days Rome did not count Christianity a danger to the State. Had St. Paul been brought to Rome because he was guilty of sedition, he would have been thrown into prison and thence haled swiftly to the judgment seat. But for two whole years he was allowed to dwell in a private house he had hired. Were he even suspected of treasonous views, he would not have had liberty to receive visitors and to instruct them. Yet this was granted him without question. And so he spoke to all, not of politics, not of Cæsar's empire, but of the kingdom of God. There, in Rome itself, though technically a prisoner, he was allowed to teach, "no man forbidding him." After all, St. Luke's artistic sense did not fail him at the close. There could scarce be an apter or more impressive finish.

And here these notes on the Acts must end. If already it has had more than its share of my space, it is because I believe that this is the book which, of all the New Testament, the general reader is most apt to undervalue.

III

We pass to the Epistles. Let the reader forgive me for beginning with a truism—namely, that an Epistle is a letter, not a collection of detached maxims. Obvious as it seems, this fact is not always remembered. A stray sentence from an Epistle is cited in argument—or used, it is to be feared, as a " text " in the pulpit—without regard to its setting. Again, the use of short extracts from the Epistles in the Liturgy would be well enough if the hearers were familiar with the whole book from which the few sentences come. But that is not to be taken for granted in our own days. On the fourth Sunday in Lent, for example, members of the English Church hear an extract beginning abruptly : " *Tell me, ye that desire to be under the law, do ye not hear the law ? For it is written that Abraham had two sons, the one by a bond-maid, the other by a free-woman. But he who was of the bond-woman was born after the flesh ; but he of the free-woman was by promise. Which things are an allegory; for these are the two covenants; the one from the Mount Sinai, which gendereth to bondage, which is Agar. For this Agar is Mount Sinai in Arabia, and answereth to Jerusalem which now is"* . . . and so on. What meaning does it convey to the average congregation? Or what, indeed, to the average reader at home? He probably, after one bewildered look, turns from it to another page, in the hope of finding it more intelligible.

There seem to be, in fact, two ways of reading an Epistle. One is to pass swiftly over its more abstruse portions, troubling neither about them nor about the general theme, content with the wise sayings and paragraphs of lucid eloquence which are scattered through it. This is as though a letter from an unknown hand should come to us, the most of it in a handwriting hard to decipher, but with a few sentences plainly written here and there. Then, having read these and found them of an uncommon quality, we desist, without taking pains to make out the rest, or indeed, to discover what the letter is about or why it was written. Yet if we treat an Epistle in this casual fashion, we can scarce believe that we gain full enjoyment from it. Moreover, we are likely enough to misinterpret such parts as we have read, because we have taken them apart from their context. The other, and far wiser, way of reading an Epistle is to study it all, learning when and why and in what circumstances it was sent, and what was the main truth which its writer wished to enforce. When once we have done that, the letter is more likely to give us true enjoyment at each future time when we return to it, or hear a portion of it read aloud.

Of course the New Testament Epistles vary much in difficulty. The Galatian letter, from which comes the extract I have quoted, seems at a first reading particularly obscure. With it we may contrast the letter to the Philippians. Here are individual phrases and allusions that need explanation, and one verse, concerning the self-limitations of Christ's nature, which carries us into the deepest places of theology. But the general drift and purpose are evident enough. St. Paul is detained at Rome, awaiting his trial. Epaphroditus has brought him a rich present from the Philippian church. While in Rome he fell ill, and news of his illness has alarmed his friends at Philippi. But now he is better, and on the point of returning home. Therefore St. Paul takes the chance of sending a letter by his hand. It has three purposes. First, he wants to thank the Philippians for their gift. Secondly, he wishes to give them his news.   As yet he does not know for certain what the result of his trial will be.   Were it his condemnation and departure from this world, he would be well pleased.   Yet he expects acquittal and release.   Then he will visit Philippi again. In the meantime, he plans to send Timothy. And, lastly, he has heard through Epaphroditus of petty squabbles which mar the life of the Philippian church, especially between two of its women members.   So he writes to enforce the need of unity.   With this general knowledge of its purpose, then, we can sit down to enjoy the charm of the Philippian letter—the happiest, the most radiant, of St. Paul's writings.

IV

As there are twenty-one Epistles in the New Testament, an attempt to consider each would make the rest of this chapter little more than a breathless catalogue.   Instead, I suggest to the reader that we take just one more Epistle and apply to it that method of preliminary survey which, I believe, is essential to getting real enjoyment from it.   The Galatian letter which I have mentioned already will serve well enough for our example.   It is short; it is as " difficult " as any;

an understanding of it gives us the key to some abstruse passages in other books, particularly in the Epistle to the Romans.

Into our hands, then, comes this ancient document. A first glance shows that it is a veritable letter—not a theological essay thrown into letter form, like Hebrews or Ephesians, but a letter written hastily at a particular moment because certain things had happened. And a mere look at the style shows we are not to find here tranquil meditation (as in 1 John) or calmly reasoned advice (as in James). Whatever may be the news which has caused this letter to be written, obviously it has filled the writer with excitement and dismay.

We begin, then, with the usual questions: Who wrote it? To whom was it written? Why was it written? The replies to the first and second are clear. Even the German critics, whose fixed idea is that no New Testament book can be written by the man whose name it bears, have for once to make an exception, and to recognize in the Galatian letter the authentic work of St. Paul. And for answer to the second question, it is enough to say that the letter was written to the Galatian Church. With the experts' interminable controversy over the rival " Northern " and " Southern " Galatian theories the general reader has no need to concern himself.

To answer our third question we must remember that St. Paul's fiercest opponents were not the pagans outside the Church, but the " judaizing " party within it. St. Paul strove to Christianize Judaism. These men hoped to judaize Christianity. In other words, they maintained that the new creed might be tolerated only if it were made subordinate to the old. Baptism must not displace circumcision. " Righteousness " must mean still a rigid observance of the Rabbinic code. The Law must dominate the Gospel. None but the circumcised, taking from the Rabbinic version of the Law both their system of worship and their guide to conduct, could hope to find favour with God.

These opponents of St. Paul followed him from place to place in the hope of undoing his work. Their usual method was to wait until he had left, and then, using the moment of reaction, to assail the converts he had made. This they did in Galatia. St. Paul's mission there had been most successful. The Galatians welcomed him with vast enthusiasm. They would have been willing, in his own phrase, to pluck out their eyes for his sake. (Was the " infirmity of the flesh " which, he says, detained him in Galatia some form of eye-trouble?) He left in the happy belief that he had founded a strong Galatian church. But scarcely had he gone before his opponents set to work. They chose two points for chief attack. First, they denied St. Paul's right to teach. He was no true Apostle, they urged. He was not one of the Twelve, and had no commission from God. What he knew of Christianity he had picked up from others, whose pupil and subordinate he was. He had no right to claim apostolic authority. Moreover, he was a " man-pleaser," who varied his doctrine with his audience.

Secondly, his teaching in Galatia was false. It belittled the Rabbinic law, in exact obedience to which lay man's hope of salvation. A large proportion of St. Paul's converts to Christianity were persuaded by these arguments, and reverted to the observance of Jewish rites and ceremonies which, at his bidding, they had abandoned. Some dismayed friend hurries to St. Paul with this news. He hears it with astonishment, anger, and grief. He must let these Galatians know his mind plainly and at once. He bids his amanuensis take pen and parchment. In words passionate with remonstrance and entreaty, in sentences that tangle themselves in their stress of emotion, he dictates— dictates the letter that we read to-day as St. Paul's Epistle to the Galatians.

Have we not bettered our chance of appreciating it rightly by reminding ourselves of facts which gave it birth? With these in our memory, let us look at the letter itself. Before St. Paul can re-state his teaching he must reassert his right to teach. He must vindicate his Apostleship. *"Paul, an apostle—not of men, neither by man, but by Jesus Christ and God the Father"*—with his first words he is in the thick of the fray. He shows the grieved amazement which the news from Galatia has given him. In a few contemptuous words he brushes aside the slander that he cares for popularity. But he devotes two chapters[1] to establishing his right to teach as an Apostle. So far from being the pupil of the Twelve, he was barely known by sight to most of them. So far from being their subordinate, he took his own line at a meeting in Jerusalem, he opposed St. Peter publicly at Antioch. In the second two chapters he re-states his doctrine of justification by faith, which may not be reconciled with his opponents' belief in justification by observance of the Law. For a few minutes (iv. 11–20), he breaks off this argument in order to make a moving personal appeal to the Galatians. Then he returns to it, and we are at the passage quoted

---

[1] I need hardly say, perhaps, that there were no " chapters " or " verses " in the letter as St. Paul sent it, or that these divisions should be ignored as far as possible when we read it. They are useful only for purposes of reference.

above as likely to perplex its hearers. *"Tell me,"* it begins, *"ye that desire to be under the law, do ye not hear the law?"* But now its point is clear. St. Paul is meeting his judaizing opponents on their own ground. They account the Old Testament supreme? Well, then, let them listen to an argument based on Old Testament analogies. It is, to be frank, an argument which must strike us as extremely forced and unconvincing. That does not matter. What matters is that this was the kind of argument most likely to influence the people whom St. Paul addressed.

Thus the first two chapters are, for the most part, personal; the second two, doctrinal. And the last two are practical. Here the writer shows what must be the results in life and conduct of accepting his doctrine. Towards the end he takes the pen from his secretary. It is his habit to put down a few sentences in his own writing, that they who receive the letter may be sure of its authenticity. In large emphatic capitals he scrawls again the main point of his message, and "See," he says, "in what big letters I am writing to you with my own hand!" And as he closes, worn out with strain, his mind returns to the irony that he, of all men, should be accused of rating popularity before God's truth. "Henceforth" (so we may paraphrase his last words)

" let none trouble me with this slander. My body, scarred by persecution, can witness of what Master I am the slave. May His Grace be with your spirit, brethren." Our Authorized Version misses the point that " brethren " is the last word of the Epistle—a last word which itself is an appeal to the Galatians, a last word to take the sting from a letter of sharp reproach.

Does this business of a preliminary survey seem irksome? I am sure it is worth while. I am sure that we cannot enjoy an Epistle as we should until we have grasped its general purpose and character. When once that has been gained, the knowledge will remain. Whenever we will we can return to the Epistle and find great pleasure in it. Charm of style, aptness of phrase, large thought, shrewd sense, eloquence, kindliness, humour—all these things we shall enjoy, as we come back to this or that letter of the New Testament collection. But to gain a clear sense of each letter's main idea—that must come first. The kind of method which I have tried, however imperfectly, to illustrate with the Galatian letter—one of the most difficult—is the kind of method we should apply to the others. Like it or not, this is the only road which can bring us to real enjoyment of an Epistle.

V

I add a few notes on some of the other books. To understand Galatians will be, as I have said, a considerable help to understanding Romans. Through much of that magnificent letter St. Paul is again combating the arguments of " judaizers." The last chapter of Romans, by the way, is more probably a separate document, attached to Romans by mistake. It is a little letter of commendation given to Phœbe, which she took not to Rome but to Ephesus, where St. Paul had a host of friends. He would be unlikely to have so many at Rome, which as yet he had never visited.

We have only a part of St. Paul's correspondence with the Corinthian Church. In our 1 Corinthians the Apostle refers (v. 9, etc.) to an earlier letter of his, which is lost. Then, between 1 and 2 Corinthians, he had to write, as 2 Corinthians tells us, a "sorrowful letter," complaining of some great wrong done by a member of the Church at Corinth. Again, every reader must notice the sudden change of tone and style when he reaches the 10th chapter of 2 Corinthians. Chapters x–xiii are quite different from chapters 1–ix. Possibly, of course, St. Paul may have had news from Corinth while he was writing which caused him suddenly to pass from approval to denunciation. Yet, if so, we should expect him to mention the fact, instead of leaving his change of tone unexplained. It seems more likely that chapters x–xiii are part of another letter to Corinth, and it is just possible that they are a part—though the less important part—of the " sorrowful letter " mentioned above. We may conclude, then, that St. Paul wrote four or five letters to Corinth, and we may be glad indeed that 1 Corinthians has survived. For that enshrines, as the reader scarce will need to be reminded, two of the most superb things in all literature—the chapter on the resurrection, and the eulogy of love.

1 Thessalonians is of special interest as the earliest of the Epistles, and probably the earliest book of the New Testament. We shall notice in it how strong is the expectation of our Lord's speedy return.

The title of " Ephesians " is misleading. This seems to have been a circular letter, addressed to all the Churches in Asia Minor. Probably it is the copy sent to Ephesus, with its special greetings, which, indirectly, has come down to us, and in this way the mistake arose.

The authorship of Hebrews is quite unknown— and quite unimportant. This is a carefully written essay, not a hurried outpouring of emotion like Galatians. It abounds with happy phrase and subtle thought. " Being dead, yet speaketh," " a great cloud of witnesses," " entertaining angels unawares " are some of the turns of speech which have passed from it into our common talk. We should notice, too, the extraordinarily felicitous definition of " faith "—and that other, more brief, of " hope." This is named " the anchor of the soul "—and the full aptness grows clear as we remember that hope, like the anchor, rests on the unseen. I must not try to discuss here the religious teaching of this wonderful book. But the more closely we examine it, the more clearly we shall realize how kindred is its point of view with the best thought of our own time. The Epistle to the Hebrews is pre-eminently a book to enjoy. So, in a different way, is Philemon— that little private note which, as unexpectedly as happily, found a place in the Bible.

Criticism has been particularly active over the shorter Epistles. From quite early times, indeed, the Petrine authorship of 2 Peter was questioned, and the case against it is convincingly strong. Elsewhere the critical judgments should be taken as tentative. Many of them find their chief support in supposed discrepancies of idiom. Unhappily some critics, profoundly expert in such details, do not seem to know literary genius when they meet it. And the argument from style or language is unsafe, if it stand alone. Style is a more sensitive, a less stable thing, than academic gentlemen suppose. It changes with mood and theme. A writer may have favourite mannerisms, words, tricks of speech at one time which afterwards he puts away. Even some trivial chance of the moment may change his diction. Suppose, for instance, that we ask a critic versed in the literature of the nineteenth century to name the author of a letter containing this sentence :

" O what a nocturient, cacaturient crew has issued of the lens of the sun of the mind on the lower facts of life ! "

he will reply swiftly, " George Meredith "; and he will be right. Then offer him another letter, written in this fashion :

" My girl and I, with Miss Macpherson her friend, went to St. Ives, Cornwall, for a month, where I took a house to be near the Leslie Stephens, where we had excellent bathing," etc.

He may not guess that this also is Meredith, and that the two letters were written within ten days.

And when we have to consider the authorship of such a letter as the second Epistle to Timothy, I would lean on the judgment of a general reader equipped with literary taste rather than on that of the scholastic critics. They, for the most part, deny that St. Paul wrote it, mainly on linguistic grounds. Some, however, deem it a sort of pastiche, including what they like to call " Pauline elements." Let the reader go through it and decide for himself. His literary instinct will reject the composite, " Pauline element " theory as incredible. The whole thing hangs together perfectly. It abounds with small personal details that ring true. It closes with one of the noblest and most moving farewells ever penned. If this be fabricated, we have to suppose some unknown writer of a genius akin to Plato's.

For I am now ready to be offered, and the time of my departure is at hand. I have fought a good fight. I have finished my course, I have kept the faith.

Yes, we shall still believe, I think, that these words come not from the study of some literary artist, but from a Roman prison, and that in them we hear, for the last time, the authentic voice of St. Paul.

I

On a lone height we stand, withdrawn from the
world. Clouds swirl heavily about us; through
their dark folds races and shifts a gleam of blood.
The ground quivers beneath our feet. Low
thunders roll ominous. Through space sound
august voices in question and answer, heavy with
doom. We hear, too, the stir of wings; through
the murk see strange figures, hurrying this way
and that. Then trumpets blare, and are still.
Suddenly over the disordered tumult falls peace.
Like riven curtains the clouds part. Beyond
them far, infinitely remote yet crystal-clear,
shines the pure City of God. At its heart stands
the Throne, clustered by adoring angels and the
exultant multitude of the redeemed. But scarce
have we begun to gaze with eager longing before
the vision is shadowed; the divine hymn faints
into returning thunder. A horror of thick darkness prisons us again. . . .

Is not this, or something like it, our feeling as we

read the last book of the New Testament? Awe
it stirs in us, and dismay sometimes, admiration
often, perplexity almost always—but can we turn
to it for enjoyment? A lofty idealism mixed
with bloodthirsty cravings for revenge, Christian
thought, Jewish legend, pagan myth—all these
we discern in its bewildering pages. In what
sense can we enjoy them?

Trying to answer this question, we must admit
that many readers have drawn from the Apocalypse a pleasure mistaken—or worse. They were
mistaken who interpreted its imagery with crude
literalism, taking pleasure in it as a guide-book to
Heaven, precise in every detail. Worse than
mistaken were they who found in some evil figure
of the Apocalypse an exact prediction of a person
or a party they disliked, and rejoiced to think that
for these the destined end was the lake of fire.
How often, and with what ingenuity of numerical
proof, has " the Beast " been identified ! Through
age after age devout folk continued this business
of finding congenial fulfilments for supposed
prophecies. Midway through the last century,
for example, the author of some quite scholarly
lectures declares that he can state the meaning of
the " unclean spirits like frogs " (xvi. 13). One is
the Reform Bill of 1831; the other is the Trac-
tarian Movement. More lately still we have been

invited to believe that all the chief characters and events of the War were prefigured exactly by the Apocalypse.

At least it can be said positively that to use the book in this fashion is a blunder. There is, and probably always will be, a large element of mystery in it, because it abounds with allusions to which we have lost the key. But its general scope and character have become clear. Formerly it was thought to be unique in literature. Now we know that it is but one example of the very many " apocalyptic " books written between 200 B.C. and the close of the first Christian century. Of those surviving, we have one complete specimen in our Old Testament—Daniel, the date of which is 240 years later than Malachi. Chapters xxiv–xxvii of Isaiah probably are also Apocalyptic. Another example, 2 Esdras, is in the Apocrypha. The Testaments of the Twelve Patriarchs, the Book of Jubilees, Enoch, Baruch, the Assumption of Moses, and the Shepherd of Hermas—the last-named being wholly of Christian origin—are important works of the same class.[1]

Apocalyptic began when prophecy ceased. Its influence was greatest in the 450 years that separated the last of the prophets from the Birth

[1] Excellent translations of some of these are published by the S.P.C.K. at low prices.

of Christ. The main purpose of its writings was to bring hope in days of trouble. The readers are bidden to expect in the near future a sudden manifestation of God, a final judgment of the wicked, the punishment of Israel's oppressors, the creation of a new and heavenly Jerusalem. "Lo, I come quickly" is a note common to them all. Their pages are full of imagery designedly mysterious, of cryptic numbers, of angels, dragons, strange monsters, horns, vials, seals; with half-veiled allusions to Temple ritual, to national traditions, to folk-lore.

Of these books, the Apocalypse of John,[1] which closes our New Testament, is possibly the last and certainly the greatest. But the others are kindred to it, and it is because these have been brought to light and studied that in modern days we can understand, as our predecessors could not, the Apocalypse of John. Like the others, it was written in a time of sore trouble; like the others, its message of comfort lay in the prediction of speedy deliverance. It was wholly a tract for the times. So far from supposing himself to unveil events of ages far distant, the writer believed that all his prophecies would be fulfilled before the first century was over. And that,

[1] "Revelation" is, of course, simply the Latin equivalent of "Apocalypse."

probably, was within ten years, for there is now a general agreement among scholars that this book was written about A.D. 90, in the reign of Domitian.

This was a period of extreme trial for the Church. Nero's hideous persecution, some thirty years earlier, had been confined to Rome itself. But now Christianity was proscribed throughout the Empire. The Master's bidding to render to Cæsar what was Cæsar's and to God what was God's had a new significance. In the old days Cæsar had claimed only the tribute, which was his. Now he claimed worship, which was God's alone. All who refused to worship the Emperor as divine were regarded as enemies of the State, to be exiled, or imprisoned, or put to death. No wonder that under this intolerable strain many went back from the faith. But, as there seemed to be no help in man, the writer of the Apocalypse was the more certain that God would intervene, and that His intervention would be of the kind pictured already in earlier Apocalyptic. More tribulation there must be first, yet soon the last of the woes would be over, and the destruction of the hated Roman Empire, with all its hideous enormities, would " shortly come to pass." At the end, there waits a new heaven and a new earth ; saints and angels exult together over the fall of Rome and of Satan.

Such, briefly, were the conditions in which this strange book was written, such the motive of its writer. As the Apocalypse of Daniel had been designed to keep the Jews true to their faith under the persecution of Antiochus Epiphanes, so this much later Apocalpyse of John strove to hearten the Christians when they were attacked by Domitian. Remembering these things, we shall find the book easier to understand. Many of its details will seem cryptic still, but we shall be able to discern its writer's main idea, and purpose, and point of view. The great power of evil which he pictures in various forms—as, for instance, "Babylon," and "the Beast"—is the Roman Empire. Sometimes "the Beast" means, more particularly, the Emperor. The Christian had no need to enter pagan temples, where alone the worship of the usual gods was practised. But he needs must pass the statues of Cæsar set up in public places, so that we understand the menace of the edict to which the Apocalypse refers, "that as many as would not worship the image of the Beast should be killed." The Beast whose number (666) "is the number of man" is, almost beyond doubt, Nero. The cryptograph which conceals his name would baffle Roman officials, but be understood easily by Jewish readers. There was a wide belief that Nero would be reincarnated as " antichrist," with whom a last battle must be fought.

Immense time, labour, and learning have been spent in considering the authorship and structure of this book; without, however, reaching decisions which can be accounted final.   But these problems, fascinating though they are to the student, may be put aside, I think, by the general reader.   The authorship of the Fourth Gospel is, as we have seen, a question he must face.   The whole value of that book depends upon the answer.   The real issue, however critics may try to blunt it, is whether we have in it fact or fiction.   Its worth cannot be the same whether its story of our Lord's life comes from the memoirs of an eye-witness or from some unknown writer's imagination.   The value of the Apocalypse, on the other hand, seems unchanged if we believe the " John " who wrote it to be other than St. John the Apostle.   The title adopted in our English Bible, " St. John the Divine " (*i.e.*, theologian), is, of course, not part of the original book.   In that we are told only that the writer's name is John, that he is a fellow-sufferer with the Churches he addresses, and has been exiled to Patmos, apparently, because he had borne faithful witness to Christ.   The evidence of style and language is heavily against the view that the Fourth Gospel and the Apocalypse come from the same author. Yet evidence of this kind is not decisive. It is confirmed, however, by the feeling of the book, by the impression it makes on us as we go through it. Such is, at least, my own experience. When I read the First Epistle of St. John, I seem, beyond question, to be in touch with the same mind as that which gave us the Fourth Gospel. Quite a different feeling is caused by the Apocalypse. Apart altogether from the contrast of idiom and vocabulary, I feel that the mind beneath this book is swifter, more incisive, less contemplative and less profound than the mind of the Fourth Gospel's author. And not easily can I attribute to the Apostle of love these pæans of fierce rejoicing over the destruction of enemies. Yet—despite the dogmatic assertions of some scholars—we cannot consider this question of authorship definitely settled, and it is not one which matters greatly, one way or another. Whether the son of Zebedee or another wrote these pages, their enduring quality is the same.

Again, the general reader hardly needs to trouble himself with the very intricate controversies that have raged over the structure of this Apocalypse. Is it, as some think, a composite work? Or is it the product of a single writer? If so, has he himself taken fragments from other writings and incorporated them in his own? Or, once more, was the book revised and extended after the days of its original author? A recent and extremely learned critic [1] is not merely sure that there was an editor, but offers us his portrait in unflattering detail. He was:

" profoundly stupid and ignorant; a narrow fanatic and a celibate, not quite loyal to his trust as an editor; an arch-heretic, though, owing to his stupidity, probably an unconscious one."

Belief in him, however, enables us to dismiss any sentence in the book which dissatisfies us as

[1] Dr. R. H. Charles, in the *International Critical Commentary*. Those who hesitate to accept his ingenious theories as incontestable facts are not to be thought ungrateful for his erudition and wonderful industry. He, beyond any other individual scholar, has restored to us the enlightening treasure of Apocalyptic. Canon Glazebrook's *The Apocalypse of St. John* (Murray) is a short and popular exposition of Dr. Charles' commentary. Valuable also is Dr. A. S. Peake's *The Revelation of John*. (Holborn Press.) Even better for the general reader who, without a knowledge of Greek, wishes to study this part of the New Testament in detail, is *The Apocalypse of John*, by Professor Beckwith, of the New York Theological Seminary. (Macmillan.) And to non-technical readers, who desire a clear and balanced statement about the position of each New Testament book in the light of modern knowledge, I cannot recommend too strongly *The Evolution of the New Testament*, by J. E. Symes. (Murray.)

" unquestionably interpolated." Suppose, for example, that we attempt to read the last chapter of John's Apocalypse under critical guidance. Verses 1 and 2, we are assured, belong to chapter xx. Verses 3, 4, and 5 should be " restored " to the middle of chapter xxi. Verses 11, part of 18, and 19 have no place in the book, being " interpolations." Then the verses which remain of chapter xxii are to be read in this order: 6, 7, 18a, 16, 13, 12, 10, 8, 9, 20, 21.

Of course the intricate elaboration of these theories is no proof that they are unsound. They may be entirely right. But, because they are apt to be stated rather dogmatically, the general reader who meets them should bear in mind that they are but theories, to which rival theories are opposed. Therefore he will be wise who remits them to the technical experts, himself contented with this book's magnificence as sacred literature.

How, then, is he best to enjoy the Apocalypse? Let him resolve, at the start, to read it in large portions, not delaying too long over verses the significance of which seems hopelessly obscure. Yet these will have become few, because he has in mind the circumstances in which the book was written, the purpose it was framed to achieve.

When to this knowledge he adds an alert sympathy, he will be unhindered by difficulties of another kind, which may have troubled him in the past. When, sitting at ease, we viewed this book simply as an abstract piece of the New Testament, probably enough we were repelled by its frequent note of fierce denunciation. But if we remember its origin, and compel ourselves to imagine what life held for a follower of Christ in Domitian's days—to what tortures and what deaths he saw his children or friends consigned, because they would not renounce the Faith—we shall not blame overmuch the writer because at times he found a savage joy in the thought of divine vengeance upon Rome. And against these passages we shall set those noble anthems of praise which passed from the Apocalypse into the loftiest worship of the Church. We shall delight, too, in the superb pictures of the heavenly Jerusalem, with their rich prodigality of detail. Are they too material? Perhaps they are for us; certainly they are if we insist on interpreting Eastern imagery with Western literalism. Yet we may remember to how many generations of believers they have given comfort; how many sufferers have found sure comfort in lifting their eyes to that far City:

" Jerusalem, my happy home,
      When shall I come to thee?
  When shall my sorrows have an end?
      Thy joys when shall I see?

  Thy turrets and thy pinnacles
      With carbuncles do shine;
  Thy very streets are paved with gold
      Surpassing clear and fine.

  Thy houses are of ivory,
      Thy windows crystal clear,
  Thy tiles are made of beaten gold—
      O God, that I were there ! "

Yes, it was this Apocalypse, beyond any other
book in the Bible, which helped countless men
and women to feel that Heaven was real.

Again, reading these pages we shall note how
clearly their writer discerned a truth of undying
value to every age, and to our own not least.
He took the right view of history. No doubt,
his visions were unfulfilled. God was to work out
His purpose in ways very different. But what
mattered incomparably more than the failure or
fulfilment of his prophecies was his serene certainty
that behind history there is God, that human
destiny is not left to chance, that the divine
scheme, though by ways past man's understanding,
is ever moving towards its full accomplishment.

Who can say that this belief, and the happy courage which springs from it, are not among our chiefest needs to-day? Or who, feeling this, and meeting the triumphant faith which shines from its every page, can fail to find enjoyment as he reads the Apocalypse of John?

CHAPTER VII   OLD TESTAMENT
                          NARRATIVE

I

MOST of us who take up the Bible for private
reading turn far more often to the New Testament than to the Old.   Plainly, it is a right choice.
The New Testament, from every point of view, is
incomparably the more important.   Often, too,
a knowledge of the New Testament will equip us
best for appreciating rightly the Old.   Beyond
question, none can read the New Testament too
much.   Yet many read the Old Testament too
little.   Their neglect of it is deliberate.   They
are haunted yet, perhaps, by ancient prejudice, by
displeasing reminiscences of schooldays.   Just
as those early struggles with St. Paul's missionary
journeys cause men still to look doubtfully
towards the Acts, so the Old Testament is linked
in their minds with class-rooms and the Plagues
of Egypt and the Kings of Israel and Judah.
For the rest, they believe themselves to know well
(through the Prayer-book version) the Psalms;

also the stories of Genesis and those of David and Elijah. The Prophetical books stand in their thoughts for clouds of obscure rhetoric, pierced now and again by some sentence of radiant beauty. . . . This sketch does not wrong, I think, the Old Testament knowledge possessed to-day by many people of a quite considerable culture. And it has this for compensation, that reading the Old Testament may bring us, apart from other pleasures, something of the joy of discovery. We may find immense delight in parts which hitherto we have left almost unexplored.

As the Old Testament and the Apocrypha fill considerably more than two-thirds of the Bible, I must not attempt to discuss separately each of the books which compose them. Instead, I shall make some general suggestions for reading with enjoyment these parts of the Bible, and say something of books, or parts of books, which probably are among the less familiar. I have ranged the Old Testament documents, for the sake of convenience, under the headings of Narrative, Poetry, and Prophecy, but it will be understood that this division is not exact. It was the practice of Hebrew writers to insert prose interludes in their poems, and to place lyrics, copied from song-collections, amid their prose narratives.

Is it quite needless to begin by insisting that the Old Testament *is* the Old Testament? For there are people who allow themselves to be seriously perturbed because they do not find the Christian standard of ethics in these pre-Christian writings. Most of the " moral difficulties " cease to perplex, and the " repulsive details " no longer repel, when we remember that this is a collection of early Oriental writings, brought together for Oriental readers. It does not lose that character because it is part of our Bible. We must not withhold from our Bible-reading that power of imaginative sympathy which we bestow readily enough on other early literature. When we turn, for instance, to *The Arabian Nights*, we are not startled because its code of behaviour differs (shall we say?) from that approved by the London County Council. One deftly written narrative, the Book of Esther, which has a place in the Old Testament, is very like an *Arabian Nights* story. Martin Luther expressed a frank wish that it did not exist, because it " contains many heathenish improprieties." Of course it does, and that is the fact which gives the book its chief value. It is not, in the usual sense of the word, a " religious " book at all. There is no mention, or thought, of God in it. Once a year the Jews kept the convivial, and quite secular, feast of Purim. The Book of

Esther was written to give an account, historic or fictitious, of this feast's origin, and to extol Esther as a national heroine. It is a splendid piece of writing. The dramatic surprises of the story are handled with a wonderful craftsmanship. But what must be our verdict upon Esther herself? We can admire her courage. She risked her life by entering the king's presence unbidden, because only thus was there a chance that her people might be saved. With noble brevity, "*I will go in unto the king,*" she said, "*which is not according to the law; and if I perish, I perish.*" But, having gained her plea, she was not content that the plotter against her race, with his ten sons, should be put to death. She persuaded the king to authorize a day's slaughter of his Persian subjects in which (according to the story) nearly 75,000 were killed. At the end of this day the king asks if she has any further request to make. She has; it is that on the morrow the Jews in the capital city may enjoy yet another day's massacre: "*If it please the king, let it be granted to the Jews which are in Shushan to do to-morrow also according to this day's decree.*" And she has her wish.

This is, of course, merely an extreme instance of a " difficulty " confronting us rather often in the Old Testament. We remember the hideous treachery, as it seems to us, of that other national

heroine, Jael; we think, too, of the slaughter of
the Amalekites, and other such incidents. If we
choose, we may take comfort from the indubitable
fact that the Hebrew standards of conduct were
far higher than those of the nations around them.
Yet it were wiser to welcome these frank chronicles
of deeds which, rightly judged culpable for ourselves, brought the doers exultation rather than
shame. For they show us, as nothing else could,
how slow was man to learn God's lessons. They
show us a people struggling upward, with many a
slip. And they show, above all, how overwhelming was the change wrought by the coming of
Christ. What He taught was no mere product
of evolution. It was not the best of Judaism
developed to a point higher than had been reached
before. It was a new thing. It brought new
hope, new ideals, new power of reaching toward
those ideals. So far, then, from misliking, we
shall prize those Old Testament pages which
show by contrast how wide a gulf lay between
the best pre-Christian theories of conduct and the
doctrine of our Lord.

II

We pass to a lesser point. When we remember
that these old chronicles were not written with an

eye to twentieth-century readers, we shall not complain because "many chapters of the Bible are simply lists of names." There is no reason why we should read them. There is every reason why we should not, for it would be sheer waste of time. But there was ample reason why these lists should be made and enshrined among the historic records of a patriotic race. To us they mean nothing. But they meant very much to the Hebrews of two thousand years ago. And, as someone has well said, if we want to know what the Old Testament means, we must try to understand what it meant. That is true of the New Testament likewise. "*Of the tribe of Juda were sealed twelve thousand ; of the tribe of Reuben were sealed twelve thousand ; of the tribe*"—why not say once for all that twelve thousand of each of the twelve tribes were sealed? Because this measured roll-call stirred the heart of Jewish readers like a trumpet, as our own may be stirred when the names are read, regiment after regiment, of an army which did mightily in our day of battle. It shows a sad lack of sympathy if we wish the Old Testament clear of such lists. They are far from valueless. They help us to understand the Hebrews' pride of race. But we should err again if, like our ancestors, we felt constrained laboriously to plod them through, because they are " in the Bible."

If, indeed, we are to enjoy reading Old Testament narrative, we should accustom ourselves to omit passages that break the thread of the story. Each of the early books is not the work of one author, but a compilation of various documents by various hands. Often, therefore, we meet different versions of one incident, or the narrative of one writer is broken off, to be resumed after a long interpolation from another source. Let us suppose, for example, that we wish to read the story of Israel's journey. At the beginning of Exodus xix we reach Sinai. And there we stay. We are told that a cloud covered the tabernacle, and the people were not to go forward until it was taken up. The later chapters of Exodus are filled chiefly by laws and ceremonial ordinances. So is the entire book of Leviticus, which follows. Most of these minute enactments are quite without interest for us, and, anyhow, our concern is with the journey. We wait for the cloud to lift. We pass on to the book of Numbers, only to find more pages of ceremonial and legislation. But suddenly, in the middle of chapter x, we read :

And it came to pass in the second year, in the second month, on the twentieth day of the month, that the cloud

was taken up from over the tabernacle of the testimony.
And the children of Israel set forward.

—and so at last the travel-story, broken off in
Exodus, is resumed. To practise the art of wise
omission in reading these early books is of great
importance. We need, in fact, to reverse the work
of their compilers, and to read one strain of
narrative at a time, undistracted by others.

We shall find this the easier, I think, and shall
follow a method bestowing other gains if we
approach the Old Testament more often as biography than as history. Then, in place of saying,
" To-night I will read part of Genesis "—or a book
of Samuel, or Kings—we shall say, " To-night I
will read the Life of Abraham "—or Joseph, David,
Elijah, Hezekiah; any of the magnificent word-
portraits with which the Old Testament abounds.
Our study will centre on a person rather than on a
period. It was thus, of course, that the narrative-
books grew. First there would be separate
stories about a great man, passed from father to
children by word of mouth. Then these would
form a written cycle. Finally, an editor would
collect a number of these story-cycles into a book.
When we read a biography, we shall omit what
is extraneous to it. We wish to enjoy, let us
suppose, the Life of Elijah. Even in the Old

Testament there is scarce anything more picturesque, anything told with more intensity of dramatic force. We shall find this Life in chapters xvii, xviii, xix, xxi, of the First Book of Kings, and in the first two chapters of the Second Book of Kings. We shall leave out chapters xx and xxii of 1 Kings, because their stories do not belong to the Elijah-cycle, and from first to last he is not mentioned in them. By concentrating in this fashion on the Life of Elijah we shall gain a clearer impression, and more pleasure, than if we mingled other stories with it, or left it unfinished because we had reached the end of 1 Kings.

In the memoirs of Nehemiah—which really are a part of the Book of Ezra, and should be so printed—we have a fascinating piece of autobiography. It shows us the man himself; an ardent patriot, fervently religious, very self-satisfied, very autocratic, tireless as an organizer, ruthless as a reformer, whose courage tramples down opposition and gets things done. Let anyone who desires a fine piece of reading try the Story of the Rebuilding of the Wall. It stands at the beginning of the book of Nehemiah, ending with verse 15 of chapter vi. (Chapter iv should be omitted; this records merely the names of the men who took part in the work.) When Nehemiah reaches Jerusalem and decides to attempt the rebuilding of the wall, his enemies ridicule his plan. He wastes no words upon them, then or later. *" The God of heaven, He will prosper us. Therefore we his servants will arise and build."* Presently they plot to entrap him, saying that they desire to meet him for conference in one of the villages. Four times they send, and each time have for reply : *" I am doing a great work, so that I cannot come down. Why should the work cease whilst I leave it and come down to you ? "* Finally, a false prophet assures him that his life is in danger, and that, for safety's sake, he should spend the night in the temple, behind locked doors. *" And I said, Should such a man as I flee ? and who is there that, being such as I, would go into the temple to save his life ? I will not go in."* Could we wish for anything finer than the intrepid scorn of those words ? So the great enterprise went forward, and the bearers carried their burden with one hand, and held their weapons with the other, *" and the builders, every one had his sword girded by his side, and so builded."* An unforgettable picture, matched by how many of a like quality in the Old Testament narratives !

III

It were needless to extol pages that became dear to us in childhood; the " Creation " and " Fall " stories—so delicately imaginative in form, so true in fact—and those of Abraham, Jacob and Esau, Joseph, Samuel, David and Jonathan, and many another. Yet always when we return to them we find something new to compel our admiration. And there are pages to suit our every mood, whether it be for a tale of action, like Gideon's, or a tender idyll, such as the Book of Ruth supplies, or for a scene heavy with doom, as we shudder beside Saul at Endor—a scene fit to rank with *Macbeth*. All these are in books we may know well, but we should not disregard others that seem unpromising. Much of Deuteronomy, for example, lacks interest, yet the farewell speeches attributed to Moses, with their measured and majestic oratory, are superb. It is when we read them aloud, perhaps, that we appreciate best their greatness. They do not break and sparkle like rivulets of popular eloquence. Rather they roll forward like a broad and even river, with a quiet but tremendous force. There are many readers, I think, who have a fair knowledge of the

Old Testament yet seldom turn for enjoyment to these great chapters of Deuteronomy.

Both here and elsewhere we shall taste gratefully the noble English of our translation, and linger to study the skill with which it is contrived. I have suggested already that we should read the New Testament in the Authorized Version, the Old in the Revised. Here the Revised keeps the beauty of rhythm and diction unspoilt, while it clears the sense, and distinguishes poetry from prose. But in one important detail the reader himself should amend both Versions. We shall have noticed that the usage of both in the Old Testament is often to print the word " Lord " in small capitals. When so printed—but not when it stands in ordinary " lower-case " letters— it represents the Hebrews' most sacred name of God—Jehovah—or, to be pedantically accurate, Yahweh.

And to keep this in mind is important. We shall misread the Old Testament continually unless we remember that Jehovah was before all else a national God—was thought of as the " God of Israel," just as a " Baal " was the God of the Phœnicians, and " Chemosh " the God of Moab. " *Among the Gods there is none like unto thee, Jehovah,*" the psalmist sang (not " O Lord "); " *there is not one that can do as thou*

144

doest.'' The great scene on Mount Carmel was, in the eyes of Elijah and all who witnessed it, a contest between two national Gods—the God of the Hebrews and the God of the Phœnicians. Which was the true God? *"If Jehovah be God, follow him,"* cried Elijah; *"but if Baal, then follow him."* Then he prayed to the God of his nation : *" O Jehovah, the God of Abraham, of Isaac, and of Israel, let it be known this day that thou art God in Israel. . . . Hear me, Jehovah, hear me, that this people may know that thou, Jehovah, art God."* And the fire came down from heaven, and all the people said : *" Jehovah, he is God ; Jehovah, he is God."* That meaning is implicit, of course, in our versions, yet it should be made explicit. The translators seem a little sanguine when they expect every reader to bear in mind that the same word must be given widely different meanings according to the type used for printing it. If we replace this rather odd typographical symbolism by using the name " Jehovah " where it stands in the original, many a passage in the Old Testament narratives will gain in vividness.

This chapter might stretch itself into a volume, for as yet it has offered but scraps of counsel, glanced for a moment at a few treasures taken almost casually from a multitude. Yet so best, perhaps, it may achieve its purpose. That it will have gained if it heartens a reader here and there to explore the Old Testament narratives more thoroughly for himself, and to learn by happy experience how satisfying is the enjoyment they can give.

CHAPTER VIII   OLD TESTAMENT POETRY

I

FIRST we must know what it is, because the poetry which a Hebrew wrote has no likeness to the literature, ancient or modern, which we distinguish at sight as " poetry." Not only does it lack both rhyme and regular metre, but its rhythms are of a kind used often in prose. The writer of English may find that one of his sentences has in it an unintended rhyme, or that another has shaped itself into a line of blank verse. But these, if he has any care for his art, he condemns as blemishes, and hastens to expunge. In Hebrew, on the contrary, so alike are the forms of verse and prose, that often we may not easily be sure whether we are reading the one or the other. Elsewhere poetry is a form more or less artificial, devised at first partly because it was easy to sing and partly because it was easy to memorize. But Hebrew poetry is simply a slight adaptation for literary purposes of a habit of language—a habit caused by the natural bent of the Hebrew mind.

Technically, the basis of Hebrew poetry is "parallelism." Commentators expound this elaborately, bidding us observe how it is to be subdivided into "synonymous parallelism," "antithetic parallelism," "constructive parallelism," and so forth. The general reader can be aided, I hope, to discern the chief features of Hebrew poetry without recourse to these impressive terms, or to the intricate analysis founded on them. Valuable as they are, these studies seem often to assume that "parallelism" was an artificial device, invented as elsewhere the sapphic stanza or the sonnet were invented. But I venture to suggest a simpler origin for it. It grew naturally, I believe, from the peculiar mental habit of the Hebrews, from their weakness for the "second thought."

Let that be put more plainly. A point of Old Testament style that must impress everyone who examines it is the enormous frequency of the word "and". The sentences consist of a series of statements, with very little use of relative or subordinate clauses. The Hebrew lacked the power of sustained thought which Greek and Roman had abundantly. Greek and Roman were able to "think out" the matter of a sentence before they wrote it, arranging what they wished to say in main and subordinate clauses. Thus the finished sentence became a work of art, in which perhaps a number of thoughts were co-ordinated, with each given its right degree of importance. Of this skill the Hebrew was incapable. He could not carry his mind forward, or deal with more than a single idea at a time. His mode of expression was to make a direct statement. To this he would add another, linking the two with " and " or " but ". To emphasize the first, the " second thought " often would repeat the idea of the first in other words. Sometimes this second separate sentence would amplify the first, expanding it or giving it a wider application. Sometimes the second sentence would modify the first, by stating an opposite truth. Such, in its simplest form, is " parallelism," and parallelism, that natural turn of Jewish phrasing, is the basis of Hebrew poetry.

A few examples may make this clear.

(A) The second sentence virtually repeats the first :

> *The king sent and delivered him,*
> *The prince of the people let him go free.*

> *He made him lord also of his house,*
> *And ruler of all his substance.*

> *I will sing unto the Lord as long as I live :*
> *I will praise my God while I have my being.*

(B) The second sentence amplifies the first :

All kings shall fall down before him,
All nations shall do him service.

Give the king thy judgments, O God,
And thy righteousness unto the king's son.

(C) The second sentence presents the opposite truth :

The Lord knoweth the way of the righteous,
And the way of the ungodly shall perish.

The waves of the sea are mighty and rage horribly.
But yet the Lord who dwelleth on high is mightier.

Such are some of the simplest forms of parallelism, from which others more complex were developed. At times the thought is continued through several sentences before the answering sequence is reached. Sometimes it is set out in a stanza of alternating lines :

Except the Lord build the house
Their labour is but lost that build it ;
Except the Lord keep the city,
The watchman waketh but in vain.

Occasionally each line carries the thought a little further than the last, so that they move forward like the successive waves of an incoming tide :

The floods are risen, O Lord,
  The floods have lifted up their voice,
  The floods lift up their waves . . .

To Sisera a spoil of divers colours,
A spoil of divers colours of embroidery,
Of divers colours of embroidery on both sides.

This, used sparingly, is a most effective device. Some of the Psalms are " acrostic "—that is to say, each verse begins with a different letter of the Hebrew alphabet, in due order. In the long 119th Psalm each of the eight verses in the first section begins with " aleph " (A), each of the second section with " beth " (B), and so on. It is not easy to reproduce this scheme in English, but an attempt was made in a book published some twenty years ago. The translator achieved his task readily enough in the earlier sections. The second, for example, began :

By what means shall a young man cleanse his way ?
  Thy word must e'en his canon be.
Betimes I heartily Thy presence sought,
  nor Thy commands would errant flee.
Because Thy words are hid within my heart
  I shall not give offence to Thee,"

and so on. The " O " section was more difficult. It began :

Oscillating minds I execrate,

151

but it was with the " Q " section, inevitably, that the struggle became really severe. This was its fashion :

Querkened, I gasp for breath, and sweet relief
  in Thy commandments comes at last.
Quemeful and kindly, turn Thy face on me,
  as aye on them that love Thee well.
Queachy my foothold—

at which point one reader at least felt that his foothold was queachy indeed, and, querkened, gasped for breath. Still, this was a courageous effort to assist the English reader in realizing the structure of the acrostic psalms.

Yet, when he knows its main principle [1] of " parallelism," the reader will learn best to appreciate Hebrew poems by reading them aloud, for their characteristic rhythms are perceptible enough even in a translation. To gain their due effect, he must give full value to the central division of a verse, making there a long pause, and one shorter, yet quite perceptible, at any subdivision. Thus let him read aloud slowly, with an alert ear, these verses, and the charm of their measured cadence will be felt :

---

[1] In its fully-developed form, Hebrew poets made use of other literary devices also, such as " assonance." But the effect of these, unlike that of parallelism, is lost in our Bible translations.

The law of the Lord is an undefiled law |
*   converting the soul ||*
The testimony of the Lord is sure |
*   and giveth wisdom to the simple.*

The statutes of the Lord are right |
*   and rejoice the heart ||*
The commandment of the Lord is pure |
*   and giveth light unto the eyes.*

The fear of the Lord is clean |
*   and endureth for ever ||*
The judgments of the Lord are true |
*   and righteous altogether.*

That is Hebrew poetry.

II

The extracts I have quoted from the Psalms are taken from the Prayer-book version, because this is probably the best known and certainly the most rhythmical. But it is also the least accurate. This cannot surprise us if we remember that it comes to us from the sixteenth century, being part of the " Great Bible," and that it was translated not from the Hebrew, but from the Latin of the Vulgate, which in turn was translated from the Greek of the Septuagint, which was translated from the Hebrew of the original. In so round-about a journey from Hebrew to English inevitable blunders were made. Therefore the reader will find it exceedingly worth while to improve his understanding of the Psalms by consulting the Revised Version of 1884.[1] Afterwards, if the Prayer-book version is used in his place of worship, scores of its verses will have a new significance for him—will, indeed, have a clear meaning for the first time. Almost any page will give an example. Let us find one near the beginning of the Psalter. On the first morning of a month an Anglican congregation sings cheerfully, as part of the fourth Psalm :

Thou hast put gladness in my heart : since the time that their corn and wine and oil increased.

Yes, but what does this mean? " They " in the Psalm, as its earlier verses prove, are the wicked. Why should the Psalmist exult because—or since the time that—the stores of the ungodly have increased? Perhaps the average churchgoer asks no question, but, meeting an obscure sentence, hopes for the best and plunges ahead. Yet the Revised Version makes all plain :

[1] For this purpose nothing could be better than the " Parallel Psalter " published by the Cambridge University Press, in which the three translations of the Psalms—Prayer-book, Authorized Version, and Revised Version—are printed side by side.

Thou hast put gladness in my heart,
More than they have when their corn and their wine are
*   increased.*

The joy which Jehovah has given His servant
exceeds that which worldlings know even in
harvest-time—proverbially the season of gladness.
Thus a moment's glance at the Revised translation
shows the verse to have a clear and picturesque
sense, which will not be forgotten when we hear
this Psalm again. And this is but one instance
from a multitude.

I shall not attempt to say much more of this
book, the supreme gift of Old Testament poetry.
To offer words of mine in praise of the Psalms
would be impertinent; to attempt an estimate of
them as literature would be impossible. The
mood of dispassionate criticism cannot be ours
when we approach writings so sacred, so intimate,
so enriched with tender and noble memories.
They who have read Hooker's *Ecclesiastical Polity*
will recall how his equable and judicious prose
takes fire for once when he speaks of the Psalms.
A part of what he wrote shall be copied here, in
place of any tribute less worthy :

" What is there necessary for man to know, which
the Psalms are not able to teach? They are to be-
ginners an easy and familiar introduction : a mighty
augmentation of all virtue and knowledge in such

as are entered before, a strong confirmation to the
most perfect amongst others. Heroical magnanimity,
exquisite justice, grave moderation, exact wisdom,
repentance unfeigned, unwearied patience, the mys-
teries of God, the sufferings of Christ, the terrors
of wrath, the comforts of grace, the works of Provi-
dence over this world, and the promised joys of the
world to come, all good necessarily to be either known
or done or had, this one celestial fountain yieldeth."

May not that suffice? What need have we to
perturb ourselves over questions of the Psalms'
authorship? The most of them cannot have
been written by David; some few may have been.
Often verses would be added to an early poem by a
later hand, to make it more suitable for use in
public worship. If the fifty-first Psalm, for
instance, be indeed David's cry of penitence, its
closing words, which long for a re-building of
Jerusalem's walls and the restoration of Temple
sacrifices, must come from another writer. As
for those sentences—how small a proportion of the
whole!—which dismay us by their pitiless in-
vective, they need merely remind us that we
are reading the Old Testament, not the New.
And when we take a larger look, how trivial seem
all such details! As we think of the myriad
souls whom the Psalms have helped and
strengthened and consoled, when we feel how
this inimitable music has pulsed through successive

ages and brought each into touch with the unseen
—why, then, our quibbling comments, our bland
eulogies die down.   Enough to bare our heads and
revere.

III

The Book of Proverbs is one which the general
reader is apt to neglect.   Often, I think, its title
misleads him.   He imagines the book to be of one
texture throughout. He finds that a proverb is
too often a moral platitude, such as :

A good man shall obtain favour of the Lord,
But a man of wicked devices will he condemn,

and it seems unlikely that a book made up of such
sayings will prove very interesting.   That is true
enough, yet a closer look at Proverbs will show that
it does not lack variety.   To begin with, it is
professedly a " composite " work.   It holds two
collections of proverbs attributed to Solomon—
the second said to have been collected by " the
men of Hezekiah king of Judah "—two short
groups of " sayings of the wise " ; the " words of
Agur," containing the famous prayer " *Give me
neither poverty nor riches* " ; the " words of King
Lemuel," and, finally, a poem—written in
elaborate " acrostic " form, and therefore later,

probably, than the others—in praise of the virtuous woman. As for the proverbs themselves, if some of them are but sententious statements of the obvious, others are extraordinarily shrewd. The sayings about " hope deferred," " he that spareth his rod," " a soft answer," " a multitude of counsellors," " a dinner of herbs," with some others, are frequent in our use, while such a thumbnail sketch as :

There is that feigneth himself rich, yet hath nothing ;
There is that feigneth himself poor, yet hath great wealth,

is as recognizable to-day as when it was made.

But, oddly as it may sound, the proverbs are not the best thing in the Book of Proverbs. For this the reader must turn to the magnificent 8th chapter, where Wisdom is set forward as a living figure who " cries aloud." (The poem is continued in chapter ix, but it should be noticed that verses 7–12 do not belong to it, being a most unhappy interpolation from another document.) The splendour of this lyric will delight the reader— and amaze him, if he have supposed all the Book of Proverbs to consist of dry aphorisms. Let me quote a part. Wisdom speaks :

The Lord possessed me in the beginning of his way,
Before his works of old.
I was set up from everlasting, from the beginning,
Or ever the earth was.

When there were no depths, I was brought forth,
When there were no fountains abounding with water ;
Before the mountains were settled,
Before the hills I was brought forth :
While as yet he had not made the earth, nor the fields,
Nor the beginning of the dust of the world.

When he established the heavens, I was there :
When he set a circle upon the face of the deep :
When he made firm the skies above :
When the fountains of the deep became strong :
When he gave to the sea its bound,
That the waters should not transgress his commandment :
When he marked out the foundations of the earth :

Then I was by him, as a master workman,
And I was daily his delight,
Rejoicing always before him ;
Rejoicing in his habitable earth ;
And my delight was with the sons of men.

Now therefore, my sons, hearken unto me :
For blessed are they that keep my ways.
Hear instruction, and be wise,
And refuse it not.

Blessed is the man that heareth me,
Watching daily at my gates,
Waiting at the posts of my doors.

For whoso findeth me findeth life,
And shall obtain favour of the Lord.
But he that sinneth against me wrongeth his own soul.
All they that hate me love death.

Well, that seems to me so glorious as to silence
comment ; a thing to be read, and felt, and

enjoyed. But if we love noble literature, are we to neglect a book which holds work of this quality?

IV

I need add but few words on the remaining books of poetry in the Old Testament. We shall not wonder that Canticles was given a place in the Scriptures only after long hesitation, and then merely because it was thought to be a Song of Solomon. It seems, in fact, to be made up of fragments from Eastern love-songs, and in its present shape it contains a few quite beautiful passages and more that seem hopelessly obscure. Persistent efforts have been made to read some sort of allegory into it, and a truly remarkable attempt of this kind is brought before us by the chapter-headings of the Authorized Version. Other interpreters, of an opposite school, have tried to find a connected drama running through the book, but their theories—which differ widely— are unconvincing. After all, is any elaborate explanation needed to fit this book for its place? If we have here but a group of marriage-songs, is their eulogy of a pure wedded love a thing unseemly in the Bible, or a teaching unsignificant to-day?

Five monotonous and very artificial poems make up the Book of Lamentations. Deeply as they must have appealed to the Hebrews for whom they were written, to most modern readers they bring less either of spiritual profit or literary charm than any other poetical book in the Old Testament.

Different, indeed, is the Book of Job. If I do not try to examine it here, this is for the double reason that no few sentences can do it justice, and that even they who turn seldom to the Old Testament at least read Job. Its majestic language and rhythms, its dramatic force, its insight, its bold front towards life's darkest riddles—these are but some of the qualities setting Job among the greatest things in all literature. One word of practical counsel may be given. To enjoy the Book of Job we must read it—not by preference, but of necessity—in the Revised Version. As Dr. Bradley, Dean of Westminster, said with truth when that Version was new :

" In reading any version of a book of such extreme antiquity the reasonable reader will be prepared to meet with occasional or even frequent difficulties. But in the older version of the book of Job, these patches of obscurity and darkness, these quagmires, if I may vary my metaphor, of unintelligible speech, do more than interrupt the reader's progress. They break up, again and again, the whole thread and argument. . . . To-day the reader has no longer a

L

collection of moving and magnificent passages broken
by intervals of unconnected and inarticulate utter-
ances, but a series of chapters the argument of which
is clear, systematic, and intelligible.''

The words were spoken in the first of his *Lectures
on Job*, published by the Oxford Press. There
have been many other expositions of a later date,
but I know none quite equal to these lectures.
The book is out of print, unhappily. But the
reader who can find a copy in the second-hand shop
or the·public library has a rare delight before him.

CHAPTER IX

I

THE prophetic books of the Old Testament are among the best reading in the world. Their religious message is of unweakened value. For background, they have scenes of eager life at critical moments of history. Their diction ranges from an alluring simplicity to heights of noble and passionate eloquence. They rouse, they teach, they fascinate. We are mistaken indeed if we leave these books unread, or fail to enjoy reading them.

To gain that enjoyment fully, we must know who the prophets were and what their tasks. Our ancestors supposed them to be merely channels through which divine predictions were passed to the ears of mankind. Later, it was seen that the prophet is not concerned chiefly with—in the usual sense—prophecy, and that prediction is merely incidental to his message. Then these men were conceived of as remote mystics, appearing suddenly from time to time, speaking at large lofty reproof or meditation, and then again living silent and apart. Yet this view was as false as the other. The prophet was neither an impersonal oracle nor an oracular person. He was a most practical man of his time. He spoke, not into the air, but to particular people at a special crisis. He spoke, not to lecture on religion in general, but because certain things had happened and others were threatened. He spoke because the times were out of joint, and he believed—an Isaiah most readily, a Jeremiah, most reluctantly —that God had called him to put them right, or, at least, to try to amend them. Before all else he was a religious teacher. His implicit faith in God was the basis of his every argument. But he applied his religion to a multitude of public affairs. Sometimes he was the trusted counsellor of kings. Always he was a politician and a social reformer. Foreign and domestic policy, national defence, the agrarian question, housing, wages, the rates of usury, the need of purity in the law-courts, the danger of formalism in worship— such were some of his themes. And he kept an eye on smaller points of social usage. Isaiah had **very** plain words to say about the feminine fashions of his day. Zephaniah condemned people who bought their clothes in foreign lands.

To understand writings so topical, we must understand the times in which they were written. The compilers of the Bible, it must be owned, have not helped us in this matter. An ill-judged regard for symmetry made them arrange the prophetic books, as they arranged the letters of St. Paul, not in their chronological order, but simply according to their length. Their method was merely to place the long books first and the short books last, irrespective of their dates. This is as though we wrote a history of England in which the sovereigns were placed according to the duration of their reigns, so that we should find the times of Elizabeth and George III chronicled near the beginning of the volume, those of William IV and Edward VI near the end. And the custom of ranking the prophets as " major " or " minor " has misled many readers. The " minor " prophets were thus labelled merely because they wrote shorter books, not because their work was less important. And two documents have been included through a misunderstanding. Daniel, as I have mentioned in a previous chapter, is not prophecy but apocalyptic, written long after the prophetical books. Jonah is not a prophetical book, except in the sense that it tells a story of which a prophet is the chief character.

There is one further point of the kind which the

general reader must note, though he need not trouble himself with details of technical criticism. The book of " Isaiah " is made up of two distinct parts, the second of which is about two hundred years later than the first. The writings of Isaiah himself are contained in the first 39 chapters. Chapters xl–lxvi come from other sources. It is convenient therefore to distinguish the two collections as 1 Isaiah and 2 Isaiah. In the former, the exile of Judah still lies ahead. In the latter, it is present, and nearing its close. Even in our English translation the change of style from chapter xl onwards is very evident.

Amos and Hosea belonged to the kingdom of Israel, which ended with the fall of Samaria about 722 B.C. All the others were prophets of Judah, and their work covers a period of some 300 years : —before, during, and after the Exile.

II

With this dull but necessary preface, and using the evidence of 2 Kings side by side with the records of the prophetical books, we can picture for ourselves these three periods, and realize the setting in which the work of the prophets was done. The first is a time of great prosperity, especially for the southern kingdom of Judah. A vast change has come to it within the last hundred years. Instead of being a self-contained poor agricultural community, it is in close touch with other nations and has developed an extremely lucrative trade with them. A century ago Jerusalem was, so to speak, a mere market-town. Its small shopkeepers merely catered for the farmers and herdsmen who came up to it at feast-times from the villages. Now it is an important business city. We hear many languages as we walk its crowded streets. Its leading men, outside the Temple precincts (the Cathedral Close, as it were), are merchants with a large export trade. A few thoughtful people are anxious about the political situation and the attitude of Assyria, but almost all the talk is of money. Honesty is out of fashion; *" making the ephah small and the shekel great, and dealing falsely with balances of deceit "* is proof of the astute and admired business-man. The new rich flaunt their luxury, and the attire of their women is a thing to marvel at, while the poor are near to starvation. Those who have been tricked out of their possessions need not hope for legal redress; the courts are venal, and a litigant's prospect of success varies directly with his ability to bribe. Speculators amass property, contriving to evict the small freeholders; they *" join house to house and lay field to field."* While the poor starve, the opulent indulge themselves with feasting and revelry. The moneyed trading class which now rules has little thought for religion. Outwardly, indeed, these traders have still to respect the seasons marked as sacred in the calendar, but they do this with a growing impatience. *" When will the new moon be gone,"* they ask, *" that we may sell corn, **and** the sabbath, that we may set forth wheat ? "*

Meanwhile citizens not absorbed wholly by business and pleasure are much alarmed by the political situation. Palestine, small in area and weak in armed force, now occupies the unenviable position of a " buffer-state." North and south of it lie the two great rival powers of Assyria and Egypt. Month by month the Assyrian attitude grows more menacing. Evidently it aims at absorbing Palestine as a step to an attack on Egypt. How can this peril be met ? There is keen and bitter debate. Some are eager for a defensive alliance with Egypt. Others, like Isaiah, ridicule this policy and those counsellors who wish *" to strengthen themselves in the strength of Pharaoh and trust in the shadow of Egypt."* Yet others are for making terms with Assyria while there is time, grimly accepting for Judah the position of a vassal-state, and purchasing safety from attack by sacrificing independence.

Such, briefly stated, were some of the religious, social, and political conditions in which the earlier prophets of Judah spoke their messages. To realize this background is to find Amos, Micah, and the earlier chapters of Isaiah full of intense practical interest. What must the prophet say in these circumstances, whether he view them, like Amos and Micah, from the countryman's standpoint, or from the townsman's, like Isaiah, that leading citizen of Jerusalem? First, he must denounce in plain terms the irreligion, the greed, the corruption, the social injustices of the times. He must attack them in detail, because they are gross offences in the sight of God. Then he must warn the nation of the Assyrian menace. It is more than a menace, indeed; each prophet is sure that nothing can avert it, for its coming will be God's righteous judgment upon an unfaithful people. How futile to hope that Assyria can be stayed by bribes or to rely upon support from Egypt! Here, then, are the two chief themes of the early prophets. We shall find one or both on their every page.

But Isaiah was a shrewd statesman as well as a great moral teacher. After the Assyrian control had been established, small confederacies were formed in the hope of its overthrow. Isaiah saw that such attempts must fail. Twice he urged kings of Judah to have no part in them. Earlier than other men he noted signs of internal weakness in the Assyrian empire. Presently it would fall. Meanwhile, Judah should not entangle itself in intrigues which must mean fresh disaster. Rather let the people return in penitence to God, and await confidently the deliverance He would send. *" In returning and rest shall ye be saved ; in quietness and confidence shall be your strength."*

He gave his counsel in vain. But Assyria fell, as he had foreseen, and the Chaldæan domination took its place. Jeremiah is among the remnant left for a time in Jerusalem. Our foolish word " jeremiad " must have been coined from a vague recollection of the " Lamentations " he did not write, rather than from the prophetical book which he did. True, he sees plainly the evil times ahead. He knows that the forces of Babylon will occupy all his country. Yet he is sure that, sooner or later, God will bring back His people. He backs his belief by purchasing land at a high price, taking care that the deed of conveyance shall be kept safely. His is a book of intrepid courage, not of despair. He does not conceal unwelcome truths, and is punished for his candour. Yet when things look blackest he is sure of ultimate victory. Ezekiel was of those who already had been deported, and must sing the Lord's song in a strange

land.   His picture of life by the waters of Babylon
is extraordinarily vivid.   And, as it helps us to
realize the intense patriotism of these exiles and
all that their sacred city meant for them, we
understand the most moving sentence Ezekiel
ever wrote—the more pathetic for its stark simplicity, as of one who must set down what is to
be said without comment, lest his heart break :
" *In the twelfth year of our captivity, in the tenth
month, in the fifth day of the month, one that had
escaped out of Jerusalem came unto me, saying,
The city is smitten.*"

III

Yet, as the years of exile continued, the spirit of
the people changed.   Some, who had yearned for
a return to Jerusalem, now despaired of it ; others
had grown content with life in Babylon.   The
most glorious chapters of 2 Isaiah were written
to end both these moods.   The prophet heaps
scornful irony upon Babylon with its soothsayers,
its diviners, its worship of idols.   And he assures
the Jews that their day of restoration is near.
Thus, in a few sentences, he sums up the message
he believes himself to have received from God :

*I am the Lord . . . that frustrateth the tokens of the
liars and maketh the diviners mad . . . that saith of*

171

Jerusalem, She shall be inhabited ; and of the cities of Judah, They shall be built.

With this clue to their meaning, the reader may better enjoy pages which scarce yield to any in the Old Testament for sustained beauty and eloquence.

To the final stage of this history belong the writings of Haggai and Zechariah. The hope has been fulfilled. Many of the exiles have returned from Babylon. Yet God's temple lies in ruins. They have made new homes for themselves, protests Haggai, but neglect the house of the Lord.

This people say, The time is not come for the Lord's house to be built. Then came the word of the Lord by Haggai the prophet, saying, Is it a time for you yourselves to dwell in your cieled houses, while this house lieth waste ?

They complain that the times are hard. Yes, but the famine and drought afflicting them are the divine punishment of their neglect. Therefore let them fetch wood from the mountains and build. Six months later the prophet speaks again. The new temple, this poor thing of wood, has been begun. But some of the builders are saddened by the contrast between it and the former temple they had known. " *Who is left among you that saw this house in its former glory ? and how do ye see it now ? is it not in your eyes as nothing ?* "

Yet let them take heart and go forward. A time will come when all nations will worship Jehovah and bring their riches, their " desirable things," for the adornment of His temple. (This, and not " the desire of all nations shall come," is the real meaning of the words.) They will but give Jehovah of his own :

The silver is mine, and the gold is mine, saith the Lord of hosts. The latter glory of this house shall be greater than the former, saith the Lord of hosts ; and in this place will I give peace, saith the Lord of hosts.

And so the work was done. Ezra, who tells us that at this time Haggai and Zechariah prophesied to the people in Jerusalem, makes us sure also that their work was not vain.

And the elders of the Jews builded and prospered, through the prophesying of Haggai and Zechariah. . . . And they builded and finished it. And the children of Israel kept the dedication of this house of God with joy.

This quotation from Ezra may emphasize again a point which none who wish to enjoy their Bible can neglect. They must disregard the order in which its various parts are arranged. Here is a great event, the rebuilding of the temple after the exile, of which both Ezra and Haggai write. Plainly, we should study their writings side by

173

side.   Yet in our Bible no fewer than twenty-one
other books stand between Ezra and Haggai.

Zechariah describes the glory that shall come to
Jerusalem when its restoration is complete.   This
he does at times in visions that are mystical and
hard to interpret, at times in some simple phrase
of wonderful charm.   As yet his fellow-country-
men find it hard to believe that the captivity is
really over, that its nightmare years are behind
them.   Then, in war or exile or privation, they
were few who could endure to old age.   Then, the
Jewish children in Babylon must be kept close,
lest they be kidnapped for slavery or for evils more
hideous.   Ill-fed and terrified they were, scared
by stories of the heathen rites and human sacrifices.
But now the clouds have lifted !

*There shall yet old men and old women dwell in the
streets of Jerusalem, every man with his staff in his hand
for very age.   And the streets of the city shall be full of
boys and girls playing in the streets thereof.*

What better than this picture could we wish for
our last words from the prophets ?   Through three
so different ages they have given, one after
another, their brave witness.   They spoke un-
heeded warnings when, before the exile, Jehovah
was wellnigh forgotten, when the priests themselves were corrupt, when every kind of social
wrong was practised, when greed and luxury

possessed the hearts of men. Later, when the doom had fallen, through the tedious and miserable years of exile it was the prophets who spoke counsel and encouragement. At the last they heartened the small returning company, they caused God's temple to stand once more in the Holy City. And now they speak of bright years to come, of the City again strong, untroubled, radiant with God's blessing; a place where serene old age taps its way into the sunshine for com-placent gossip, and the streets ring with the mirth of boys and girls at play.

IV

To enjoy fully, then, the prophetical books of the Old Testament, this is the essential rule—that we realize the prophets as human beings, as most practically minded men, writing to meet special needs at special times, and that we look closely to learn what were those times and those needs. We should observe also the character of the religious teaching which was common to all the prophets. It marked a parting of ways. It was the beginning of a long and fierce controversy. On the one side was ranged the powerful tradition of the priests, strengthened by the publication, in

Josiah's reign, of the Deuteronomic code. It made ceremonialism the centre of religion. The elaborate system of ordinances and sacrifices was magnified as the one means of winning divine favour. The Law was supreme. In sharp conflict with this was the teaching of the prophets. Religion, said they, was of the heart and soul and will. Sacrifices and outward ordinances were worthless, unless they were matched by a true inward faith and resolve. We shall find this clear teaching in one after another of the prophetic books. Micah turned the Deuteronomic code itself against the priests in his splendid paraphrase : *" Shall I come before God with burnt offerings ? Will the Lord be pleased with thousands of rams, or ten thousand rivers of oil ? He hath shewed thee, O man, what is good ; and what doth the Lord require of thee but to do justly, and to love mercy, and to walk humbly with thy God ? "*

Unhappily, the re-establishment of the Temple strengthened the party of the priests. More and more fiercely they fought against the prophetic interpretation of religion. At length they prevailed. The Law, as expanded and expounded by the priests, was accepted for the sole guide to conduct. Righteousness was thought to begin and end with outward obedience to this code. Prophecy was silenced. The Old Testament prophets were to be read only in the sense given them by the priests. Further prophecy was forbidden. Through four centuries no writer dared to give religious teaching in his own name. Thus was created that view of religion against which our Lord had to contend. Never a prophet more was there, until so suddenly and strangely a voice was heard by the Jordan, speaking again like the prophets of the far past, bidding the hearers repent, for the Kingdom of God was at hand.

I

A WORK professing to speak, with whatever brevity, of " the Bible " must needs include some reference to the Apocrypha. For this collection of documents is not some kind of supplement to the Bible, but an integral part of it. The Roman Church, indeed, reversed at the Council of Trent the wise decision of St. Jerome. It declared these books to be fully " canonical," having the same degree of authority and inspiration as the rest of the Scriptures. By this decision of the sixteenth century it remains bound. We who belong to other Churches may be glad that we are un-pledged in this fashion. Yet the fact that we rate the Apocrypha, as a whole, below the rest of the Bible does not justify the printing of Bibles from which this part is omitted entirely. In the services of the English Church a good many " Lessons " are chosen from the Apocrypha. The VIth Article of Religion orders them " to be read for example of life and instruction of manners."

They may be read also, we shall find, for enjoyment.

Most of them were included in the Septuagint, the earliest Christian Bible, but excluded from the Hebrew Canon. They differ enormously in value and interest. Among them we find very naïve legends. The little book of "Bel and the Dragon" supplies an example. First Daniel, by an ancient stratagem, exposes the fraud of the Bel idol. Then the king leads Daniel to the Dragon:

Wilt thou say that this is of brass? lo, he liveth, and eateth and drinketh; thou canst not say that he is no living god: therefore worship him. Then said Daniel, I will worship the Lord my God, for he is a living God. But give me leave, O king, and I shall slay this dragon without sword or staff. The king said, I give thee leave. Then Daniel took pitch, and fat, and hair, and did seethe them together, and made lumps thereof; this he put in the dragon's mouth, so the dragon did eat and burst asunder.

Diverting enough! But it is as well that we are not required to accept this, or the stories in Tobit—in one of them Tobias so scared the devil with a smoke-ball that "he fled into the uppermost parts of Egypt"—as canonical Scripture. On the other hand, some of these books are noble literature, full of wise thought. It would be hard to maintain that reading Leviticus, which is a

canonical book, benefits us more than reading
Ecclesiasticus, which is not. In short, if he
possess it not, the reader should hasten to obtain
a copy of the Apocrypha in the Revised Version—
this is incomparably better than the other—and
he will be sure both of profit and enjoyment.

He may have remarked that my previous
chapters had no word of Ecclesiastes, that mourn-
ful book of disillusion, with a superb ending. Of
set purpose I passed it over, wishing the reader
to study it side by side with the Apocryphal
book, the Wisdom of Solomon. This was written
perhaps about the time that our Lord was born,
and almost certainly it was designed as a reply
to Ecclesiastes. As was mentioned in the previous
chapter, after the silencing of prophecy no one
was allowed to write of religion under his own
name. Hence arose the custom of associating a
new book with the name of some great man of
the past—Enoch, or Moses, or Solomon, or
Daniel. Every reader knew of this practice;
there was no attempt at literary fraud in adopting
it. Ecclesiastes was written in the character of
Solomon. Only after much hesitation was it
placed among the Scriptures. Many people read
it with resentment. It seemed to deny the
doctrine of immortality, and to counsel mere
hedonism. "Get what pleasure you may from

life, for soon it is over. One end comes to all alike, good or bad, and human existence is but vanity "—such seemed to be its message.

Therefore one reader resolved that Solomon should be identified no longer with a philosophy so pagan and so depressing. He himself would write another book in answer, and name it " The Wisdom of Solomon." In his second chapter he paraphrases the thoughts of Ecclesiastes. It begins thus :

For they said within themselves, reasoning not aright :
Short and sorrowful is our life,
And there is no healing when a man cometh to his end,
And none was ever known that gave release from Hades,
Because by mere chance were we born,
And hereafter we shall be as though we had never been :
Because the breath in our nostrils is smoke,
And while our heart beateth reason is a spark,
Which being extinguished, the body shall be turned into
*   ashes,*
And the spirit shall be dispersed as thin air ;
And our name shall be forgotten in time,
And no man shall remember our works. . . .

Not an unfair rendering, as we see when we compare actual words of Ecclesiastes :

All his days are but sorrows, and his travail is grief.
For that which befalleth the sons of men befalleth beasts ;
As the one dieth, so dieth the other. . . .
All go unto one place ; all are of dust and turn to dust
*   again.*

There is no remembrance of former generations,
Neither shall there be any remembrance of the latter
generations,

—and so forth. " *Come therefore and let us enjoy*
the good things that now are," is Wisdom's version
of the advice given by Ecclesiastes, " *There is*
nothing better for a man than that he should eat and
drink and make his soul enjoy good." All through
this second chapter Wisdom sums up the teaching
("reasoning not aright") of Ecclesiastes. Then,
with the third chapter, follows the familiar and
splendid reply to this false doctrine; beginning :

But the souls of the righteous are in the hand of God,
And no torment shall touch them.
In the eyes of the foolish they seemed to have died ;
And their departure was accounted to be their hurt,
And their journeying away from us to be their ruin ;
But they are in peace. . . .

It is, then, a study of extreme interest to read
Ecclesiastes side by side with this answer to it.
Both are nobly written, but how different is their
tone ! Already the writer of Wisdom seems to
foreshadow that other answer to Ecclesiastes
given in the first Epistle of John. " *One genera-*
tion passeth away and another generation cometh,
but the earth abideth for ever," says Ecclesiastes.
" *The world passeth away and the lusts thereof ;*

but he that doeth the will of God abideth for ever,"
is the triumphant answer of St. John.

The other great treasure of the Apocrypha is
Ecclesiasticus, " the Book of Sirach." It is one
we can take up at any time, open at any page
and be sure of meeting something which delights.
It may be a shrewd piece of practical counsel, or
general observations which retain their point,
such as :

> *Wine is as good as life to men*
> *If thou drink it in its measure ;*
> *What life is there to a man that is without wine ?*
> *And it hath been created to make men glad.*
> *Wine drunk in season and to satisfy*
> *Is joy of heart, and gladness of soul,*
> *Wine drunk largely is bitterness of soul,*
> *With provocation and conflict.*

Or we may light on a fine piece of rhetoric, like
the apostrophe to Death, or a pæan that thrills,
like that beginning :

> *Let us now praise famous men,*
> *And our fathers that begat us.*

He that does not enjoy Ecclesiasticus is hard to
content !

II

Some of the other Apocryphal books must be
mentioned briefly. " Esdras " is simply the

Hellenized form of " Ezra," and the " 1 Esdras " of the Apocrypha is identical, to a large extent, with the " Ezra " of the canonical Scriptures. As a whole it is more interesting and better written. 2 Esdras is quite different; a book of melancholy apocalyptic visions, written possibly soon after the fall of Jerusalem in the year A.D. 70. I do not think it will attract the general reader. If he likes a grim story magnificently told, he will find one in the book Judith. He knows its theme already, no doubt, but unless he has read it lately in the Apocrypha, he well may be staggered by the masterly power with which it is told there. The crowning scene, in the tent of Holofernes, is wonderful. We feel the Oriental atmosphere, the atmosphere of lust and luxury, the cool, calculating mind of Judith, who risks so much, who plots and carries through a deed so horrible, for love of her nation. Not a pleasant tale, to be sure—but the man who gave it us knew how to write.

Baruch (parts of which are included in the lectionary of the English Church) is, to my taste, rather flat and uninteresting. If we need an effective contrast to Judith, let us turn rather to the Song of the Three Children, where we find *Benedicite* in its original form—that splendid canticle which puts us in mind of St. Francis.

The two books of Maccabees possess great historical interest, and, despite some verbosity and some dull interludes, are, as a whole, good reading. The English by which they are rendered is particularly flowing and attractive. Both as a specimen of it, and for the quaintness of the passage itself, I will quote from the author's prologue to one of his sections. He explains that he has reduced to one book the ample chronicles of Jason of Cyrene, which filled five. He continues in this not unhumorous fashion:

And although to us, who have taken upon us the painful labour of the abridgment, the task is not easy, but a matter of sweat and watching (even as it is no light thing unto him that prepareth a banquet, and seeketh the benefit of others); yet for the sake of the gratitude of the many he will gladly endure the painful labour, leaving to the historian the exact handling of every particular, making no effort to fill in the outlines of our abridgment. For as the masterbuilder of a new house must care for the whole structure, and again he that undertaketh to decorate and paint it must seek out the things fit for the adorning thereof; even so I think it is also with us. To occupy the ground, and to indulge in long discussions, and to be curious in particulars, becometh the first author of the history; but to strive after brevity of expression, and to avoid a laboured fulness in the treatment, is to be granted to him that would bring a writing into a new form. Here then let us begin the narration, only adding thus much to that which hath been already said; for it is a foolish thing to make a long prologue to the history, and to abridge the history itself.

Not the best kind of writing, this, yet extremely good of its kind. And it may help to convince some readers—who have met it here, I suspect, not without surprise—how extraordinarily varied are the styles, as well as the matter, which they can find within the covers of the Bible. He would be foolish indeed who turned most often to the Apocrypha; yet he also is unwise who never examines its curious and fascinating medley of literature.

III

And here, reluctant, I must end this slight study of a vast theme. I am sure that we shall do well to take up the Bible sanguine of enjoyment, and to make it a book of frequent and familiar use. Instead of a thing set apart for rare moments, the Bible, because it is the book we rate most highly, will be also the book we read most often. And the more we read it, the more keenly we shall enjoy. Its pages are rich with thoughts of that great company unseen, with tender memories of the past. In our own day they link us with all other Christians, and there is nothing more fit to end the pettiness of religious strife than the larger vision, the true sense of values, which the Bible gives. And for the future? We wonder, and surmise, and hope—but it is when we read the Bible that, most of all, we trust. Then it is, amid whatever throng of uncertainties, that we grow most sure of a power that does not age, of a love that cannot fail.

THE END